Editor-in-Chief and Founder:
  Lyndon H. LaRouche, Jr.
Editorial Board: *Lyndon H. LaRouche, Jr. , Helga Zepp-LaRouche, Paul Gallagher, Tony Papert, Gerald Rose, Dennis Small, Jeffrey Steinberg, William Wertz*
Co-Editors: *Paul Gallagher, Tony Papert*
Managing Editor: *Nancy Spannaus*
Technology: *Marsha Freeman*
Books: *Katherine Notley*
Ebooks: *Richard Burden*
Graphics: *Alan Yue*
Photos: *Stuart Lewis*
Circulation Manager: *Stanley Ezrol*

INTELLIGENCE DIRECTORS
Counterintelligence: *Jeffrey Steinberg, Michele Steinberg*
Economics: *John Hoefle, Marcia Merry Baker, Paul Gallagher*
History: *Anton Chaitkin*
Ibero-America: *Dennis Small*
Russia and Eastern Europe: *Rachel Douglas*
United States: *Debra Freeman*

INTERNATIONAL BUREAUS
Bogotá: *Miriam Redondo*
Berlin: *Rainer Apel*
Copenhagen: *Tom Gillesberg*
Houston: *Harley Schlanger*
Lima: *Sara Madueño*
Melbourne: *Robert Barwick*
Mexico City: *Gerardo Castilleja Chávez*
New Delhi: *Ramtanu Maitra*
Paris: *Christine Bierre*
Stockholm: *Ulf Sandmark*
United Nations, N.Y.C.: *Leni Rubinstein*
Washington, D.C.: *William Jones*
Wiesbaden: *Göran Haglund*

ON THE WEB
e-mail: eirns@larouchepub.com
www.larouchepub.com
www.executiveintelligencereview.com
www.larouchepub.com/eiw
Webmaster: *John Sigerson*
Assistant Webmaster: *George Hollis*
Editor, Arabic-language edition: *Hussein Askary*

EIR (ISSN 0273-6314) *is published weekly (50 issues), by EIR News Service, Inc., P.O. Box 17390, Washington, D.C. 20041-0390. (703) 777-9451*

European Headquarters: E.I.R. GmbH, Postfach Bahnstrasse 9a, D-65205, Wiesbaden, Germany Tel: 49-611-73650
Homepage: http://www.eirna.com
e-mail: eirna@eirna.com
Director: Georg Neudecker

Montreal, Canada: 514-461-1557

Denmark: EIR - Danmark, Sankt Knuds Vej 11, basement left, DK-1903 Frederiksberg, Denmark. Tel.: +45 35 43 60 40, Fax: +45 35 43 87 57. e-mail: eirdk@hotmail.com.

Mexico City: EIR, Sor Juana Inés de la Cruz 242-2 Col. Agricultura C.P. 11360 Delegación M. Hidalgo, México D.F. Tel. (5525) 5318-2301 eirmexico@gmail.com

Now Obama Can Be Removed

A Presidential Policy Statement From Lyndon LaRouche

Oct 20—The overwhelming majority of sane Americans reacted with horror and anger at the clown show of a Democratic Party Presidential debate staged by CNN and Google on Tuesday, Oct. 13. The disrespect for the institution of the Presidency that was demonstrated by the manner in which the debate was engineered, came close to matching the obscenity that has characterized the several Republican Party debates so far.

In response to an outpouring of support that I have received, by merely speaking the truth about these abominations, I must issue the following brief statement on the nature of our current national crisis and the proper framework for approaching this vital Presidential election.

First, the defining issue for today is the fact that Wall Street is hopelessly, irreversibly bankrupt, and there can be no serious improvement in the conditions of life for the vast majority of Americans until Wall Street is shut down altogether. The first and most immediate remedy for the bankruptcy of Wall Street is the reinstating of Glass-Steagall.

The simple truth is that an honest appraisal of the disastrous collapse of real productivity in the U.S. economy, shows that a large and growing majority of our fellow citizens are facing job loss, starvation, collapse of genuine health care services, the destruction of the educational system, and an overall disintegration of basic infrastructure. This has accelerated under the Barack Obama presidency, but it began before that, particularly during the George W. Bush terms in office.

Any attempt to dodge this fundamental truth during the now-ongoing Presidential campaigns, by appealing to "issues" or populist slogans, dooms the United States to total destruction in the very short-term period ahead.

Wall Street must be shut down totally. The entire Wall Street system is bankrupt. It must be ended. Then, we must do what Franklin Roosevelt did to overcome the Great Depression. Today, we face an even greater

H.R. 381 is one of three bills ready for immediate restoration of Glass-Steagall in the Congress. It has 68 sponsors.

challenge, due, in part, to the decades of collapse of the productive powers of labor in this nation. Shut down Wall Street now, reinstate Glass-Steagall as a means of reconstituting viable commercial banking, and then begin a program of Federal credit to revive the productive economy, through capital investment in infrastructure and other vital programs. We must begin to reverse the collapse of our industrial economy, and we must train a new generation of young people to develop the skills to function in a modern, technology-intensive growing economy.

This is what the 2016 Presidential candidates must address. Any attempt to divert from this essential agenda is tantamount to surrendering to Wall Street and those who would see the United States disintegrate altogether.

A segment of the American people, horrified by the clown show of last week, is demanding nothing less. Any candidate who fails to meet this standard does not belong in the race. This is not a popularity contest, or a test of who can best pander to the worst pragmatic impulses of a beaten-down and terrified public. This is an election that will determine whether or not the United States still has the moral fitness to survive.

I hear the American people crying out for a future minus the scourge of Wall Street. They deserve nothing less.

EIR Contents

www.larouchepub.com Volume 42, Number 42, October 23, 2015

Cover This Week

Nine out of ten people killed in Obama's drone operations were not the intended targets.

Right Now, We Have Reached A Turning Point

This is the complete transcript of Lyndon LaRouche's dialogue with the LaRouche PAC Policy Committee on Oct. 19.

Matthew Ogden: Good afternoon. It's Oct. 19th, 2015. My name is Matthew Ogden, and you're watching the LaRouche PAC Policy Committee weekly discussion. I'm going to introduce the members of our Policy Committee joining us over video [from right to left]: We have Bill Roberts, from Detroit, Michigan; Dave Christie, from Seattle, Washington; Kesha Rogers, from Houston, Texas; Michael Steger from San Francisco, California; and Rachel Brinkley from Boston, Massachusetts. And here in the studio, I'm joined by both Diane Sare [of Manhattan and New Jersey], by Benjamin Deniston from the LaRouche PAC Science Team, and Mr. LaRouche.

So, we already started having a conversation, but I think we can pick it up.

Lyndon LaRouche: Yes, well, right now we have reached a turning point, which follows on what happened on the thirteenth [Democratic Presidential candidate debate], and the thirteenth was a travesty. It was an orgy, an abomination, and all those kinds of things. But unfortunately for the enemy, that is not a popular trend. And it's going to go in the other direction, and has gone. We have had in the past interval of a week, we have had the greatest increase of popular support among people who are voting or planning to vote, that we've had in a very long time.

LPAC-TV

Lyndon LaRouche discusses with the LaRouche PAC Policy Committee on Oct. 19: "We have the possibility of achievements which were not accessible to us for a long time."

And so therefore, now, our job is not to be abstract about these problems. We know that we now have put the spurs on Obama, that Obama is now finished. Everything globally says that Obama is finished. That's what's going to happen now. We find in Manhattan, and she [Diane Sare] finds in New Jersey also the same thing, a complete change from pessimism, to saying, "Well now that we've got all this success, are we going to get some money too?" And that sort of thing.

So, it's great! This is what has happened with Russia. Russia's activity has been the mechanism,—the achievement of Russia's success, and what it's still doing has been the trigger which has ignited a global ability to turn the tide in favor of mankind. And that's what we're doing! And our people have to catch onto the fact they're going to be wearing clothes now, not rags. But it's not going to come so easily.

But what I got on the past 48 hours is a striking blow: the nation and parts of the world are moving. And of course, what China and Russia have done in adding to that, has been *absolutely crucial* in this change in the circumstances of the whole planet.

So we are in a period of responsibility, not to claim great achievements, but to realize that we have the possibility of achievements which were not accessible to us for a long time. And therefore, we have to use and support those talents, recognizing that you have a responsibility to make sure that *you* make your contribution in the process which we're fighting to bring forth now.

Obama is a Killer

Ogden: Well, there are a number of items that have all sort of colluded against Obama, that are all coming to a head right now. You have the publication of what's called *The Drone Papers,* in Glenn Greenwald's publication *The Intercept,* which just thoroughly document this killer mentality that's behind this targeted assassination program using drones, that's dominated Obama's Presidency. [See *Obama Indicted,* p.16 in this issue.] You have the continuation of this Doctors Without Borders investigation into what they are alleging are war crimes,

Official Congressional photo

Former Congressman Peter Hoekstra (R-Mich., 1993-2011) was one of those to blast Obama for training and arming terrorists in Libya, during ABC-TV's Oct. 18 exposé.

with the targeted, sustained bombing of this hospital in Kunduz, Afghanistan.

And now you have everything around the Benghazi attacks coming to a head once again. Hillary Clinton is going to be called to testify. You had a major television special [by Sharyl Attkisson] on this yesterday that was published, and it goes through step-by-step the cover-up, the lies, Susan Rice's role, the role of Hillary Clinton directly, and all the way to the top, to Barack Obama. And then also a thorough denunciation of the policy of regime change, what Obama did to overthrow Qaddafi, who had in fact been working together with other people to target and eliminate the kind of radical jihadist extremism that has now taken over Libya, Syria, Iraq, and so forth.

So all of this is now coming together at the same time. And I know this is documented in a leaflet that we are distributing today in Manhattan around the vicinity of the United Nations. That's happening as we speak.

LaRouche: Yes, and this is our organization in Manhattan, it actually has become a bunch of,—I wouldn't say zealots, it's the wrong word to use,—but they've been enthusiasts. And they've been going out and taking on British leadership who park their carcasses in Manhattan. And I don't think they'll enjoy Manhattan much any more. But this is what's happening. We have a change in mood, a change in opportunity.

The problem that I see, I see in our own organization. We have some people behaving like idiots, and they are not paying attention to what the reality is. And so they still go with the pessimistic attitude they've had for a long time. When in reality, we now have reached a higher level of influence internationally than we've ever had in my lifetime.

Diane Sare: Well, I'll just say that the release, which is up on the LaRouche PAC website today as the Lead has gone viral. I mean, it's been shared, I heard, as of 9 o'clock this morning, something like 16 hundred times. We had double and triple the normal number of people who sign up for emails, signing up to get our email. And I think people in a sense have been waiting for this break. They hate Obama, but they're terrified of Obama, and they've succumbed to the pessimism. But this is irrefutable. And you did say in April of 2009 that Obama was a failed personality. You used Nero and Hitler, and the drone policy is so *precisely* a Nero kind of policy, that it is just undeniable, and at this point it's irrefutable.

And you have that, and then you have his decision to bomb the hospital in Afghanistan. The Doctors Without Borders had taken all of the appropriate measures. Their coordinates were precisely known. They called NATO and they called the United States, whatever the chain-of-command was, and said, "you're bombing a hospital," and yet we continued to bomb it for at least 45 minutes *after* that. And now that there's an investigation, we're sending in bulldozers to cover over the evidence!

So it is absolutely irrefutable, and I think there were a number of things that were very sharp at the New York meeting. One of our activists there just said that Congress should be held criminally responsible if they don't throw this guy out of office, based on what is now in the public domain. [See *Manhattan Dialog,* p.27 this issue.]

The British Ran the Show

LaRouche: We have similar things on this thing. There's the analytical approach to this. We're just describing the effect. But look at the analytical standpoint of it as well. So what happened is that the British actually ran the convention of the thirteenth.

Sare: Of the debate.

LaRouche: They ran it. I picked them up on the previous Friday; and I picked them up in the early morning session. And I found there were two teams of British operatives who were gathering around this area, to converge on this intended conference.

Hillary Clinton is now a destroyed politician. The effect has not been registered fully yet, but it will be. It's inevitable. She's finished. And several of the other people are also going to be finished, and I have to admit that I will do something which will cause them to be finished. I have some plans to do it, which I'm responsible for, and I will do that. I will engineer it.

But the thing is, what is the key

to this thing? Well, you take Valerie Jarrett. Now she's a known person; she's a British agent. She's totally British, and she's a British agent, but she runs under the idea of being a U.S. citizen. But she's not. She's a British agent. And she's the one who orchestrates the whole business of the Obama machine inside the United States. She's the one who runs it. And it was very clear in the process of the way she inaugurated her position in terms of the United States. So she's finished, for that reason.

What that means is, Obama was not a brain. That is not his character. Obama is a killer, a professional killer, with a quality of character which is characterized by his stepfather. Now the stepfather was removed from the scene, because his mother, Obama's, was frightened, even though she became quite evil and so forth, and that sort of thing. And so therefore, what happened is that Obama is an echo of his stepfather. He's a perfect model. He's a killer intrinsically. All he's done is kill, kill, kill, when you take the number of cases of people who were killed, who outnumber the number of targets by a massive degree!

So now Jarrett, of course, was a mediator of pulling Obama into the Presidency. She was the one, and she was the one that controlled it. She's British. She has a U.S. cover, but she's British. And Obama is not a thinking person. He has no real intelligence, as a thinking person. He's a killer. His whole history as President has been that of a killer. His attitude fits exactly with what his stepfa-

White House/Pete Souza

Who's ordering who? Senior Advisor Valerie Jarrett talks with President Obama in the Oval Office on May 6, 2009.

ther represented. He was a professional killer. He was such an evil killer that Obama's mother pulled Obama personally, while he was in adolescence, out of his association with his stepfather. But what stuck to him was not her influence; what stuck to Obama was that attitude.

So Obama is nothing but a mad killer. That's what he was from the beginning, and what the point is, is that the members of the United States government, agents of the United States government, allowed themselves to be drawn into a systemic kind of murder, which no respectable society will do. No one will go out with that kind of killer program. But Obama *needed* it! Obama had a *need* to do that. He had a *need* to be evil! And he is a typical Satanic figure. I mean the quality of his life, from the time he became exposed, and Jarrett is his charmer. Jarrett is the one who created him, or played a key role for the British in creating him. And the whole package of Jarrett and Obama is a gift of the British Empire.

Ogden: Well, this includes Hillary Clinton too. She was pulled into that Administration and forced to compromise herself, and now she's completely tainted by what Obama represents.

Obama's Been Flanked, But...

LaRouche: Absolutely, that's exactly it. But see, the point is, if you give in to evil, you become a member of it. And that's what happened to her. And then we have a lot of other people of the same category. And so suddenly, when Obama is challenged by what *we* have done,—we have done part of our job because we've brought him down.

Now he has not been brought down formally at this point, but the threat of what will happen to him is almost inevitable. He's gone, or will be gone. The only thing he can do is try to blow up the world. But you look how successful Putin is in everything he's doing right now, and the American leaders, the American military specialists, are really *awed* by his success. They never thought that he was going to be able to do that. And he has picked up qualifications of strategy, which the members of the United States government lack.

So this is where we are, and I think the discussion we should have, is pertaining to this point of reference.

Dave Christie: Well, Lyn, I just want to add one thing here, because *Sputnik* news this morning had as one of its top news items one of our associates in Europe, Karel Vereycken, who heads up the Agora Erasmus [in Belgium]. It was a combination of him being interviewed, and covering some of the writings on the whole deployment of the B61-12s, the mini-nukes into Europe, which obviously, are being upgraded under Obama's kill policy, the real, big kill policy. And part of what I think was being discussed earlier was,—in Seattle here, we had an event where none other than Niall Ferguson, who is a known apologist of the British monarchy, came and gave somewhat of a sleepy discussion about a book that he wrote on Henry Kissinger [*Kissinger 1923-1968: The Idealist*].

As he's sort of droning on and most of the audience is falling asleep, but in the middle of it, all of a sudden, he says, "Oh, and by the way one of the most significant things about Henry Kissinger, was his brash call for the use of limited nuclear warfare against Khrushchov, to prevent him from invading through the Fulda Gap, and... ho-ho-ho. Sort of like Putin today." I'm sitting there almost falling asleep in this thing, and then saying, "what is *this* all about?"

Then also, Fareed Zakaria, who's known to write for the establishment administrations, and so on and so forth, echoed that same call.

So I just think we should be very clear that however much Obama's been flanked, that if you leave him in there with these kind of weapons and this sort of forward basing, that's not a game that we want to play.

LaRouche: [laughs] Obviously!

Sare: I'll just say, and Rachel may have more because she was at this meeting in Manhattan, where we learned that this baron—I guess we have to give these Brits their titles—Baron Adair Turner ...

LaRouche: Oh my God! [laughter]

Sare: ...speaking on his book, called *Between Debt and the Devil*—like one is good and one is bad? I don't know—but anyway, she went, and the blurb had this little sentence at the end which made it clear to us; it said that we have to disabuse people of the notion that printing money is inflationary. Because sometimes it's necessary. I was thinking, this was exactly what you were warning that they were going to attempt to do.

And then they get there, and it's a small crowd for a large auditorium, but the head of the Bank of England is sitting there in this meeting, so obviously it was a *crucial* intervention into Manhattan. And a few things occurred, which, Rachel, if you want to say something about it, since you were witness to this activity. I don't think the Brits were too happy after that.

A Shift in Manhattan

Rachel Brinkley: Yes, the main thing—I'll try to remember all the details, but one of our members stood up while he [Turner] was giving this extremely boring dissertation, and said: "Look, I've got a question. Are you going to let us ask questions now?"

And they say, "go ahead. What's your question?"

And he said, "Glass-Steagall, what do you have to say on that?" And he ignored it; he said, "I don't have an answer to that."

And later on, she stood up, and said, "Look, this whole thing is a fraud. You come here to tell us what to do, when you have been running this corrupt system," and she attacked this British policy. She said, "We are for an American policy,"—FDR, Hamilton, Lincoln,—and they threw her out of the event; they had some problem with her saying that.

Another of our activists stood up and brought up the point that Turner had said at the beginning of his discussion that he was surprised by the 2008 financial collapse, but then proceeded to say that he's an expert on everything else that we should do now, obviously defending this debt system that's going to kill billions of people. Our activist said, "Look, you expect us to believe you when you already admitted that you had no idea what's going on in this financial system. Why don't you take your ideas back to Britain and start a pig farm with David Cameron?" [laughter]

So, it was interesting: The response in the audience—there actually were a number of questions tending towards the idea of a public credit system, because we did sort of break the façade, and you found that there was a sense underneath; and one thing people brought up is we don't just need Glass-Steagall, we need a change in the system. That was the response of one young questioner who brought up the need for a public banking system, and get rid of this whole game, although it needs to be advanced.

And another woman brought up that the only time there's been hyperinflation in U.S. history was when there was a British ship in the New York harbor that was counterfeiting U.S. currency! So, that kind of… that is a question of, "look we know what you guys are here for; you can take it home. We want an American System policy."

LaRouche: Yes! [laughter] That was very much the

Franklin D. Roosevelt Presidential Library & Museum

Franklin D. Roosevelt in his "Governor's Chair" in Albany, New York in 1930. His legacy still resonates with Americans.

tone of that, a whole bunch of Brits were there in Manhattan and they thought they had the whole thing fixed. And one of our members there, gave them a lecture; it was not somebody saying, "What d'ya think? What d'ya think?" This member got up and made a very pungent argument, which startled the Brits, and the result was, another guy, a Brit, said, "what's going on here?" And so, this thing really took over. And I think they got a lesson on that one.

But that's the direction we have to be going in; we are going in that direction. You know, you take the case of our own organization and the finances of our organization. What happens is, people get discouraged. They say, "Look, we're not going anywhere; we're not succeeding in anything; we're losing all the way back; nothing is working any more. What do we need you for?" That kind of attitude about the citizen toward us. Now, that changed suddenly. And you find that as a result of the week, between the thirteenth and now, there has been a fundamental change in the general attitude within our population itself on this issue. We have more support now, than we've had in what seems to us like a century. It may not be quite that long, but the way we experience it, is, when was the last century we got treated like that?

And that's what the situation is. So the problem is now, is not how are we going to succeed? That's not a problem. The problem is not to make a mishap of success. And therefore, we have to be very practical in that sense of using policies very carefully which fit the changing attitudes of the citizens of the United States. Now you will get the richest response in Manhattan. There are certain other spots in the United States that will also have an advantage of getting a more immediate response.

The Southern states will be more difficult, because they are not humane. And the problem is of course, the racist attitude which is reflected most expressly in the Southern party, in the area of slave-keeping, which the certain relevant, early President of the United States set into motion.

And so therefore, it's in Manhattan is the prime center for the recovery which is being presented to us as an opportunity right now. And we will find the greatest success in our immediate effort practically, will come in that way; will come from the New England area, and certain other areas, and northern California. Southern California is less of a prospect.

So now our job is to say, "well, this is what we have; these are the people; we have responses from our members and friends in this area." The report we have from this morning, I think, is really enthusiastic. So the job is now, it's nice to have enthusiasm, but it's better to have success, and success means doing some work to bring about success. While I'm very optimistic in terms of my views of what is possible, my concern is, what are my fellow-members capable of doing? Because the opportunity is there,—how ready are they to recognize what the change means, and to recognize the mission-orientation they have to not only think, but express efficiently?

We have a wonderful opportunity on this particular day, on the date of this particular meeting. It has been conferred upon us. So you have to enjoy the day, but you have to fulfill the purpose of the day. This can be good, *very* good. I'm sure that we have some other people on the roster across the board to respond on what their view of that matter is.

Eradicate the Green!

Benjamin Deniston: Well, one key reference point you've defined repeatedly in the recent period is Franklin Roosevelt. That's a model we have for the shift we need in the country right now. And correspondence in time between the release of the "Drone Papers" and the Democratic debate, I think, just highlights a lot about where the reality is, and where it's not, like this crazy, freak-show debate where they're taking turns kissing Obama's butt! And at the exact same time, you get this devastating release showing just how sick and disgusting this guy is.

But that's just showing you how far this system has diverged from reality. And it put us in a unique position, as you're saying here, to define a very unique form of leadership, to direct this nation in the right direction again. And this Franklin Roosevelt reference I think is something people can resonate with. It's part of our history, part of our culture. And it's not just a single policy or a gimmick,—it's a change in culture, it's a change in outlook. We need to return to those roots of our nation and I think that's a key reference point we have as you've defined it.

LaRouche: At this point, just to make sure we follow through on that: What we have is the nature of mankind. Now, we're working on a promissory note for mankind. We are not giving them yet, by what we've said so far, we are not giving them the solution. We're giving them a promise that the solution is available as an option.

The problem is that there's a nature of mankind and the way that mankind's existence is understood. That's where the problem runs. People do not recognize what mankind owes to the planet, what mankind owes to the Galactic System, and to related things which lie in between and around that.

Mankind is the only species which has a destiny to re-create mankind himself, to be a creative force in the universe. Now, the way this expresses itself is, ask the question: "In your society, what's the death rate relative to the number of people that live?" What are you contributing to create the future, to the ideas of the future, the things that are required for that? What do we demand of our educational system, to make this gift of opportunity given to us now, to realize the benefit?"

So, I mean, you Ben, of course, have one of the best aspects of this among us on that question. What do we mean by the Galactic System? What do we mean by the lesser parts of the same system? Where does man come into the Solar System and beyond as a factor,—where does the future of mankind lie in space, and in reaching into far distant places, like the Galactic System, or various parts of the Galactic System*s*?

And that is, if and when mankind, as when the people in our nation and in other nations, grasp that feasibility, that it's real, it's not a dream; it's a practical reality: That every generation of human beings should, as a generation, be more qualified intellectually than the preceding generation. That's the law. And therefore, if we do not emphasize that, you are ignorant of these opportunistic situations that we have now.

The only way you can do that, is actually, we've got to go to *physical* science. It means we've got to *shut down* everything that's green! All green policy must be eradicated. And the people who advocate it must be given appropriate forms of occupation. If they can pick things like bugs or various kinds of beasts off the vines and things like that; if that's the only skill they have, let them pick the bugs from the vines, and so the vines can prosper. [laughter]

But the situation is that,—because what's the problem up to now? So far, the Twentieth Century and what is now the Twenty-First Century's entry, present us with the threat of a doomed humanity. And therefore, we have to change the law, to eliminate everything in the nature of climate control, all these other fads; we have to increase the productive power, the creative power, of the human individual. We must not have a green policy. The green policy itself must be driven into death, now; otherwise we're going to fail. We're just going to make one promising note, one promising option, but then we will fall into misery. And the first thing to do is to shut down the British Empire. Because the British Empire has been one of the most efficient mechanisms, for making people stupid.

Look at Kepler and Leibniz

Michael Steger: Well, Lyn, to go back to what you said, that it's not just a question of acknowledging where we are, but also to fulfill it. Because you just made it clear: Eliminating the green policy, eliminating the British Empire, Wall Street, the whole Bertrand Russell conception and definition of man, that has to be gotten rid of.

It reminds me of Kepler's work, because what Kepler does, he not only identifies—first, he identifies that there *is* a principle, that there's a principle governing the larger system that we abide in. But then Kepler has the revolutionary quality of mind to say: OK, how does that principle fulfill itself? How does it bring itself into being as a developing characteristic? And that's where Kepler then falls upon this Classical musical conception; the Classical harmonies are actually fulfilling the principle which he can empirically acknowledge exists. And so it just stands out to say that what Kepler had demonstrated about physical science, is also

very true about mankind's ability to develop itself; as we see today with what we've done in Manhattan, and the musical takeoff there.

It's just very striking how you not only have to identify where we are, but what's the means by which mankind fulfills that potential. And this Classical musical Renaissance we see burgeoning in Manhattan, I think is only an example of what we see as the potential. We've seen it, we've seen it as a response of the population to the debate. There was a sense, "My God! There is *nothing*, there is nothing unless I do something!" Even the source to the "Drone Papers" says, it is now upon every individual who has access to this information to do something about it. And that is exactly I think what captures the moment. But the question is *how* do you fulfill that potential? And Kepler and what you have said and done, are exemplary.

LaRouche: Well, I think you go back to Kepler and before Kepler, and you will find in that process that modern society's achievements, when they were achievements,—and they weren't always achievements; sometimes they were very evil, like in the Twentieth Century. But when you look at what Kepler represents, and then you look at what Leibniz accomplished, and take those two points of reference as a secondary reference…. And also, what was done in terms of China. We're talking about Leibniz,—Leibniz's spending his efforts in the study of science in China.

And these kinds of things have been forcing processes, which represent the *essence* of the existence of the creation of the United States. Now, this has not always been harvested in a happy way. But that idea of progress,—the necessary scientific progress,—and you can call it today *scientific progress*, and scientific progress is the precondition, for the survival of mankind. Now we have an opportunity, post Obama, to proceed with that mission.

And don't be practical! Don't defend anybody who's got a green policy. Anybody running around with a green policy, should be spat upon, in a manner of speaking. We don't want to do the act of spitting, but we'd like to feel that they are being spat upon.

Deniston: And it really is a form of clinical insanity. You have two layers: You have the British Royals and their like, who just want to kill people. It's not about the planet, it's not about green, they want to kill people; they want one billion people or less, that's what it is. Then you've got those idiots who follow it, and the ironies are just everywhere.

White House video

Foreign Affairs Ministry, Denmark

The Green Mafia out to kill: Barack Obama (left), Jerry Brown (center), and Prince Charles (right).

I mean, they say they're a green movement, but the whole planet is net greener today because of CO_2, than it was 30, 40, 100 years ago: We actually have a greener planet, because CO_2 is not a pollutant, despite what Obama's EPA says; it's a plant food, that's kind of a critical part of the entire biosphere. And in historical terms, we're in what some people call a CO_2 famine. The level of CO_2 concentration in the atmosphere is actually, in geological terms, a low period, in the very low range. You get much lower and plants can't even grow.

So, we've done a relatively small increase; it's been much higher in the past, too. It's been five, ten times higher than it is now even, and we've only increased a little bit. But already that's had a net effect in increasing the total greening on the planet. People have done studies, like global crop yields have increased by something on the order of $140 billion a year, attributed to the increased CO_2 concentrations, the increase in the growth. There's all this stuff out there.

Then you get these morons are out there, campaigning against CO_2, saying this is pollutant. It is clinical mass insanity: They don't even know what they're following; they don't know what they're talking about. When you have,—the real issue is this Zeus faction which we just have to get rid of. That's the source of this thing.

So get rid of Zeus, and then we can have a lot of re-education to do, to teach people what it means to be human. Which is what I think you're talking about here.

Sare: The irony is, people who are promoting this green crap, I mean, from London, the British Monar-

chy, they're the same ones advocating that we could have a limited nuclear war! Now how great would a nuclear war be for the planet or the environment?

Higher Qualities of Existence

LaRouche: It's obvious that what Ben has just emphasized here is extremely important: The ability of mankind depends upon mankind's creating the transformation of the media around us, and transforming it into something which enriches mankind's ability! And this is on the basis of energy-flux density; which is my favorite subject, as it's been known for some many years about this thing! And probably will be known in one way or the other, in another different way.

But the point is that this principle is the principle. And therefore, we just have to make sure *that* works. But if we don't do that, then we will lose, because what will happen if the green policy is allowed to be continued, is that mankind will be destroyed. Therefore, for the safety of mankind, we have to deal with that.

We also at the same time have to add a positive element to that business, and that is true creativity. Human creativity. The important thing is that the death of a person, or the death of human persons, is not a problem for mankind. *If* the condition is that mankind is able to generate a new layer of human population, which is capable of leading members of that generation to a higher level of achievement, scientifically, of physical science than ever before.

As long as mankind is progressing, and perhaps able to get in control of the Solar System, or to get control of the Galactic System,—those are the things that define morality. And if they're lacking, then all your thing about worshipping God and so forth *ain't worth anything!* If you cannot perpetuate what the Christian principle is supposed to mean in terms of the history of mankind's progress, to higher qualities of existence, to higher levels of understanding,—without that *you are nothing!* And everyone there, including the Governor of California, should be told and reminded that he's unfit to serve in any responsible capacity as a person.

And that's the way to do it: just say, "You're a faker." I don't care who you are.

The way it will work is, Obama is going down. Now, Obama is one of the pieces of crap, which has been the bad part of the history of the Twentieth Century and now, by getting rid of Obama, we will be actually energizing and activating the progress of mankind, not to simply recover from the disasters of the past, but to remove the obstacles to mankind's progress. And without mankind's progress for the future, there is no future.

Kesha Rogers: Yes, and the obstacles to mankind's progress and mankind's creativity are Obama and Wall Street. And that's why Wall Street has to be brought down, and Obama has to be removed and impeached. And we have to actually get the population to see themselves more as citizens of the universe and of the Galaxy, and that that's where their power lies. That's where the power of the population lies in terms of getting out,—as you said very strongly on Saturday,—of this "little me, I'm the victim, I'm the slave" to "we can now transform mankind to a whole a new era, to a whole new plateau of the breakout in the progress of mankind."

And you're sitting here having to deal with the insanity of a mass killer in the White House, while the reality is that we have the potential of even greater forces coming in to wipe out the population, which we can take on, such as the threat of galactic forces, such as the asteroids, which has become once again a very prominent factor, Nations have to work together at this

Official Congressional photo

Hawaiian Congresswoman Tulsi Gabbard, a leading voice of revolt against Obama's tyranny in the Democratic Party, and murderous insanity in Syria.

point in time to make sure that we save that which is the beauty and creative powers of mankind, to free mankind from these threats and these disasters. And as long as you have these, as you said, "impediments" in the way, then we will not be able to do that. And I think we're on the verge of removing them, very quickly.

LaRouche: Except you've got to remove the Pope, this current Pope. If the current Pope were to prevail over the reign of people who are Catholic, and if they accepted what he was teaching, that would lead to the destruction of mankind. That would be a *Satanic act.* And actually a Pope who would take that policy, unless they abandoned that policy and purified themselves of their evil tricks that they picked up,—you're going to have a destruction of mankind. And therefore that Pope, and his doctrine,—either the Pope has to change, or the Pope has to be changed.

And that's a very important factor. And it's international. And if you start that kind of thing, that kind of religious doctrine, you'll get people of different religions all over the planet killing each other. And that is not going to do any good.

China and Russia Are a Moral Force

Bill Roberts: I think that's right, because it goes together with this Wall Street problem, that people believe in this mythology that there's some way that they have to survive by allowing other people to be destroyed and to be killed. And that is the slave mentality. That is—you know, someone said the slave has half a mind. We still have this subjective problem with the American population, even though the Empire is largely being brought down internationally,—the American population has to be induced to decide to be human, and decide to be human by saying "we're going to have a future."

LaRouche: Tell the Pope.

Steger: Well, Lyn, I think it's interesting, in light of this collapse of Obama and the move by Putin, that you've also seen the disintegration of both of the political parties' leadership. You've got the revolt in the Democratic Party; you have a revolt in the Republican Party. And you raised specifically this question of a Manhattan Party, a nonpartisan effort to shape the Presidency. And really, this question of both Wall Street and this green ideology,—the destruction of both of those has to be a unifying principle; also with the affirmation of a development program, but that characteristic really does defined this Manhattan question.

LaRouche: So does Russia. And so does China. China is actually a moral force relative to the devilish force of Obama and the

Putin's intervention in Syria has been trigger for turning the tide in favor of mankind. Here, a Russian plane takes off from the Hmeymim airfield in Syria.

British. Therefore, if you look at what the progress of China has been so far, and the reconstruction and resurrection and rebirth of Russia under Putin's leadership, we see it now in practice. And these are things which we have to be conscious of. Because we will have a system of nations, but these nations will not be of the kind of selfish nature that we've been taught to have. It means that we will bring what we know, in our ability and in our knowledge,—we'll bring that to use for all mankind, but especially right at home.

And beyond that, we have to create a future for mankind. Which means, what we must do, in every generation of human life, that generation of that level of life, that scale of life, that generation of life has to be superior in its creative powers to any national condition before. And that's the law: Mankind must produce generations which are creative relative to what already exists. And you must take the leadership of the best leaders, of the greatest progress of mankind and say that those people are the proper leaders in spirit, of mankind as a whole. How do you think we're going to do what Kepler thought he was going to do, the unfinished business of Kepler's achievements? What do we think we're going to do about what Leibniz did? A lot of that got forgotten in the process.

So therefore the question is, are we going to breed generations of children, and train them to bring a popu-

lation whose creative powers of knowledge and practice are greater than any previous generation? *That's our mission.* That's what it comes down to.

Will Mankind Be Allowed to Progress?

Sare: I think what you're saying about the Pope,—I immediately was thinking about what's happened with these refugees coming into Europe, and the attack on Angela Merkel, who, for once, has got something right which is her decision to accept the refugees and the humanizing effect this has had on some substantial portion of the population of Germany; where people have decided, "No, these are human beings, we may not understand their language but they are human; many of these refugees are well-educated. They have a contribution to make to mankind, and we're not going to lower ourselves to treat another human being as an animal."

And I think this is really a profound question, because I've been picking up from various emails and things here in the United States, that there's a trend among some of these Tea Party and other circles; they were getting all riled up against the immigrants. And of course, all of these problems come from Obama! I mean, he's arming and supporting the Mexican drug cartels; he's arming and supporting ISIS; he did these wars, he overthrew Qaddafi—he has caused this! But you have a very nasty, *evil* line, even in the United States now against Merkel, for her decision to accept these refugees, and I think it really is just very sinister and cynical about what it means to be a human being, and what our relationship is to the rest of mankind, therefore.

LaRouche: Well, take the Southern population, the black slavery, and similar kinds of slavery, and these are evil forces. You know the third President of the United States, who was a very evil person, Jefferson; and we had his followers, who were similarly evil. Maybe not as actively as he was. That's the same thing.

And that's the point. That we have to remove those kinds of factors of behavior in the people in the United States and in nations in general. Like [Finance Minister] Schäuble in Germany is a model case of a man who just wants to kill and eat people, out of his own problems and own frustrations, and he takes his frustrations out, with extreme bitterness, on the basis of the fact that he was crippled and injured and so forth, as he was. But he *hates* people! And you have other people in Germany who have the same problem. You have a lot of French people—the French got a lot of Nazis in there! They don't call it Nazis, but they are Nazis.

You take the history of de Gaulle, Charles de Gaulle: Charles de Gaulle escaped from the British influence,

went out and organized. What happened with Russia? If Russia had not fought as it did, there would not be a United States. Without Stalin there would have been no United States.

Ogden: Franklin Roosevelt understood that.

LaRouche: Yeah, very clearly! And other people did. But, of course, the forces in Germany were a problem, but Russia had big problems. And it was only when Russia was organized in a way which had a mission orientation, that it could do something.

Now he was killed; he was murdered, Stalin. Stalin was actually murdered. And a lot of my friends who had known of the Stalin level, leading people, they were snuffed! But this was what the kind of problem is. We have to think about the nature of the people who live,— will they allow human beings to progress? Or will they try to do everything possible to destroy the ability of the progress for mankind as, shall we say, the Creator would intend mankind to progress?

Let's win!

Ogden: All right! On that note—I think we can bring a conclusion to this discussion at this point. I want to thank everybody very much for joining me. And stay tuned to larouchepac.com.

Obama Must Immediately Be Removed From Office and Prosecuted for Murder

Oct. 17—The following is a transcript of the core of the presentation made by Jeffrey Steinberg on the Oct. 16 LaRouche PAC webcast. That webcast was hosted by Matthew Ogden.

Now the reality is that we can't wait. The reality is that Obama must be removed from office in the immediate days ahead, and this is not a matter of trying to scramble around to find some pretext in which to do that, because Matt just mentioned at the outset, that the Glen Greenwald-Jeremy Scahill new publication, *theintercept.com*, has published an extraordinary 8-part series, based on newly-leaked government documents. These documents were prepared after Edward Snowden had already dumped his material, and had already left government, and probably already taken refuge in Russia.

What these documents show, is that President Obama is guilty of mass murder. The entire drone program that has been the hallmark, the entirety, of the Obama Administration's counter-terrorism program, has been conducted outside the framework of the U.S. Constitution, outside of international law, and represents perhaps the single greatest incidence of mass murder in the modern history of this planet.

Now, that may sound extreme, but I would urge all of you to not just read the 8-part series of articles, but to go to the links to the actual documents that reveal the true nature of this Obama administration, completely lawless mass murder campaign.

One of the points that's made right at the outset, in the opening article of this series, is that since 1975—and you can go back to the history of the revelations about CIA crimes, the Church and Pike Committee investigations—during that period President Gerald Ford issued an Executive Order and laws were passed, making it explicitly illegal for the U.S. President to order assassinations. And of course, President Obama, since the very beginning of his term in office, has been regularly convening Tuesday meetings at the White

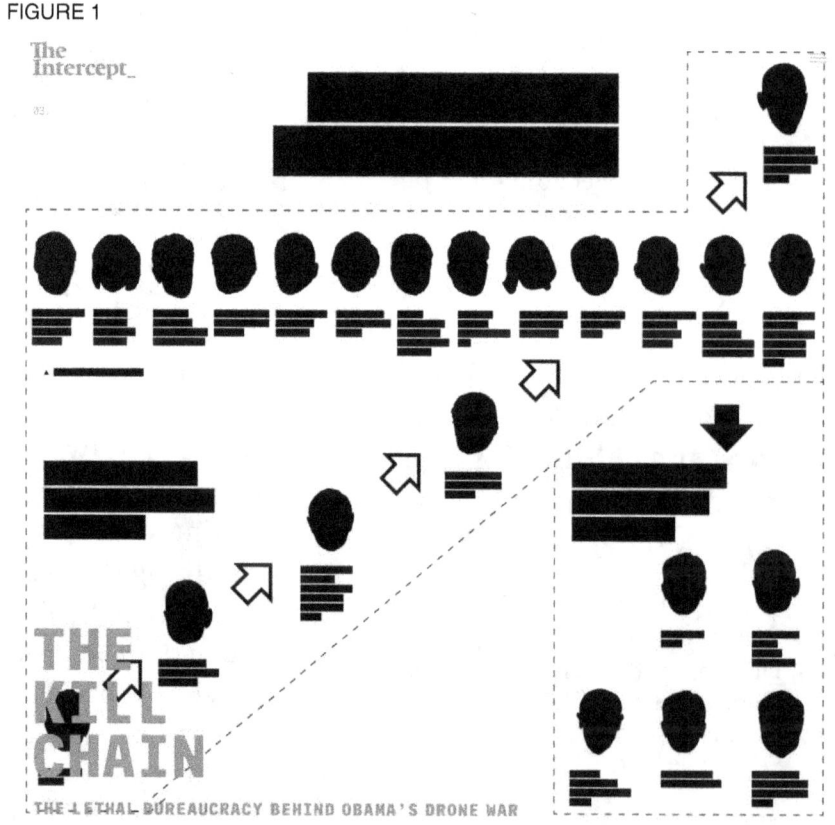

FIGURE 1

This graphic is adapted from a slide in a May 2013 Pentagon presentation showing the chain of command for ordering drone strikes and other operations carried out by the Joint Special Operations Command in Yemen and Somalia. The original can be found here.

House, where they've been specifically developing kill lists of targets to be gone after. And so, rather than use the appropriate and accurate term of assassinations, President Obama and his team choose the word "targetted killings," but the concept is identical.

We've talked on a number of occasions in recent weeks on these webcasts on Friday night, about General Michael Flynn, who was the head of the Defense Intelligence Agency and was fired by President Obama in the summer of 2014 for being a major obstacle to the kinds of illegal programs the Administration has been running since the beginning. General Flynn was interviewed by *theintercept.com* to comment on the documents and to comment on his own first-hand knowledge of this assassination program. General Flynn had been the Director of Intelligence for the Joint Special Operations Command, for Central Command (JSOC), and then became the head of the entire Defense Intelligence Agency. Here's what he had to say about the Obama Administration's program:

"The drone campaign right now really is only about killing. When you hear the phrase 'capture or kill', capture is actually a misnomer. In the drone strategy that we have, 'capture' is a lower case c. We don't capture people any more. Our entire Middle East policy seems to be based on firing drones. That's what this Administration decided to do in its counter-terrorism campaign. They are enamored by the ability of Special Operations and the CIA to find a guy in the middle of the desert, in some shitty little village (pardon my French), and drop a bomb on his head and kill him."

Doubletalk and Lies

Now to hear President Obama, you would think that the White House program has been surrounded by Constitutional lawyers who've been studying every step along the way, to make sure that everything involved in this program is legal. In a speech at the National Defense University several years ago (2013), President Obama discussed the program, and again, I quote:

The United States has taken lethal, targetted action against al-Qaeda and its associated forces, including with remotely piloted aircraft, commonly referred-to as drones. As was true in previous armed conflicts, this new technology raises profound questions about who is target-

CSPAN

Obama tries to defend his unconstitutional drone policy of mass murder in a speech at the National Defense University on May 23, 2013.

ted, and why. About civilian casualties and the risk of creating new enemies. About the legality of such strikes under U.S. and international law. About accountability and morality.

Drone strikes, he concluded, are effective and legal. Now, it happens that under pressure, particularly after news reports about his Tuesday kill-meetings at the White House, caused quite a stir, the White House issued a policy document. It's in the public record; it didn't have to be leaked out. It's called "U.S. Policy Standards and Procedures for the Use of Force in Counter-Terrorism Operations Outside the United States and Areas of Active Hostilities."

I won't bore you with the precise language of this document, but among the highlights, they say:

In every instance we prefer to capture rather than kill. We have precise standards for the use of lethal force, and these criteria include, but are not restricted to, near-certainty that the terrorist target is present, near-certainty that non-combatants will not be injured or killed, an assessment that capture is not feasible at any time of the operation, an assessment that the relevant government authorities in the country where action is contemplated cannot or will not address the threat to U.S. persons, and an assessment that no other reasonable alternatives exist to effectively address the threat to U.S. persons.

And they say:

FIGURE 2

EKIA →

Over a five-month period, U.S. forces used drones and other aircraft to kill 155 people in northeastern Afghanistan. They achieved 19 jackpots. Along the way, they killed at least 136 other people, all of whom were classified as EKIA, or enemies killed in action.

HAYMAKER Operations (01 May – 15 Sep 2012)					
Type	# Ops	EKIA	Detainees	JP	%
Enabled Ops	27	2	61	13	48%
Kinetic Strikes	27	155	N/A	19	70%
Total	54	157	61	32	

Note the "%" column. It is the number of jackpots (JPs) divided by the number of operations. A 70 percent success rate. But it ignores well over a hundred other people killed along the way.

This means that almost 9 out of 10 people killed in these strikes were not the intended targets.

theintercept.com

These statistics from Obama's "Operation Haymaker" in the Hindu Kush (Northern Afghanistan and Pakistan) document how almost nine out of ten people killed in these drone operations were not the intended targets.

There must be a legal basis for using lethal force, and secondly, that lethal force will only be used against a target that poses a continuing imminent threat to U.S. persons.

Now, the fact of the matter is that these were strict rules for targetted killing that were promulgated by the Obama Administration, signed by the President himself, and as documented in *The Intercept* series, by commentaries by people like General Flynn, this policy has been violated in virtually every instance. So even by the criteria that his own Administration set forth, President Obama has been guilty of carrying out what can only be described as mass murder.

Cause for Dismissal

Now, there are procedures for dealing with crimes of mass murder. Number one, to the extent that the President is directly implicated in these actions, this is cause for immediate and obvious impeachment, and perhaps, because of the urgency and timeliness of this, it would be more appropriate to simply invoke the 25th Amendment. If you have somebody who has been living under the cloak of apparent civility and respectable position, but who turns out to be a mass murderer, then you'd have to conclude that that person was suffering from a form of socio-pathological insanity. That invokes the 25th Amendment immediately.

And so, that's the situation that we're dealing with. What Mr. LaRouche said, is in this case, you would want to remove that person, President Obama, from office *immediately*, and then immediately commence with criminal proceedings for the mass-murders that he's committed.

No Capture, Just Kill

Now, among the documents that were leaked to the authors of this series of articles, is a document that was prepared by the House Select Committee on Intelligence in April of 2012. It was called the Performance Audit of the Department of Defense Intelligence, Surveillance, and Reconnaissance (ISR).

What this audit by the House Intelligence Committee concluded, is that the entire targetted-kill program was rife with violations, with failures to live up to any of the standards that would be appropriate under the Constitution, or even under the Obama Administration's own guidelines, and that basically there was a mad rush to try to line up as much money as possible for these drone-kill programs, and therefore there were shortcuts, there was misrepresentation of the program, and in fact since the September 11 attacks, the Defense Department has spent $67 billion on putting together the ISR infrastructure that the Obama Administration has exclusively used for the drone killing-program.

Now, other comments on this. Again, from General Flynn. He said that the White House for reasons of expediency abandoned its own guidelines. There were no attempts to capture. There were no attempts to work with local governments on setting up the circumstances to capture. There was no attempt to live up to the standard that to be a legitimate target for these assassinations, the individual had to oppose an immediate and imminent threat of terrorist attack against the United States. And General Flynn said:

> We've tended to say, drop another bomb via a drone, and put out a headline that 'We killed Abu Bag of Donuts' and it makes us all feel good for 24 hours. And you know what? It doesn't matter. It just made them a martyr. It just created a new reason to fight us ever harder.

Flynn went on to say that there was "way too much reliance on technical aspects of intelligence, like signals intelligence, or even just looking at somebody with unmanned aerial vehicles. He gave an example: "I could get on the telephone from somewhere in Somalia, and I know I'm a high-value target. And I say in some coded language, 'The wedding is about to occur in the next 24 hours.'" Flynn said:

That could put all of Europe and the United States on a high-level alert, and it may just be total bullshit. SIGINT is an easy system to fool, and that is why it has to be validated by other INTs, namely like human intelligence. You have to ensure that the person is actually there, at that location, because what you really intercepted was the phone.

Dept. of Defense/Claudette Roulo

Army Lt. Gen. Michael Flynn, the former director of the Defense Intelligence Agency (July 2012-Aug. 2014) and the former intelligence director for JSOC (July 2004-2007), gave an exclusive interview to theintercept.com blasting Obama's "capture or kill" program as "only about killing."

And in fact, one of the things that was concluded in this in-depth House Intelligence Committee review of this drone-kill program was that in most instances, there was almost exclusively reliance on the tracking of cell phones, and so, very often, it was the cell phone that was the determinant of the location where the drone attack occurred. And in many instances, almost a majority of the instances, many innocent people who just happened to be in the wrong place at the wrong time were killed, and immediately afterwards, even though these people were not known, they didn't even know what their identities were when the drone-firing took place, they would immediately be classified as unknown enemy combatants. In other words, if you were there, you were de facto a terrorist, and it was de facto justified that you were a legitimate target for Obama's assassinations.

Obama Decides Who Lives and Who Dies

Now, the documents also included a number of structural flow-charts. The point that the Pentagon and the CIA wanted to make, was that these programs did not involve a few people sitting around in a room, going through piles of what they themselves called "baseball cards"—photographs and biographical information on the people who were on the potential-target list. It was based on the data in these "baseball cards" that the President of the United States would sign the kill-order. And once the kill-order was signed—and by the way, it usually took on average 58 days from when an individual was identified by name to when he went through the process of investigation, surveillance, and his name landed on the President's desk for a finding that this person should be killed.

Then from that moment on, there was a 60-day time deadline for accomplishing the killing. I'm sure part of the reason for that is that every week there were more and more names being added, and the priorities were continuously shifting. But the fact of the matter is, that there was an elaborate chain of command through which this vetting process took place; chains of command within the military and the CIA. Then there was a chain of command which led up to what was called the Principals Committee, which are the leading members of the President's Cabinet and heads of other agencies that have critical roles to play in this process.

And then in every single instance, the ultimate decision was made and was signed off on by the President of the United States. So, in other words, every single person killed in this drone warfare program was authorized for assassination by President Obama.

Now, we know that there were a number of leading advisors, particularly John Brennan, who for the first four years of the Obama Presidency was the President's Counter-terrorism Advisor right there at the White House; then he was made Director of the CIA. We know that David Petraeus, who was formerly a high-ranking military commander, brought over to the CIA, and who was found not only to have been engaging in an extramarital affair, but was caught passing massive amounts of classified documents to his mistress and biographer; and yet he only received a slap-on-the-wrist misdemeanor, and to this day is still a key advisor to President Obama. Petraeus propagated a series of orders, establishing the chain of command and the operational profile of at least the Joint Special Operations Command (JSOC) part of this kill program.

But ultimately, everything landed on the desk of President Obama; and when he signed the kill order, the 60-day clock began to tick down, and that was when the operations in the field went into action.

Ripping Up the Constitution

We know, of course, that Anwar al-Awlaki, an American citizen, clearly someone who had an association with al-Qaeda, was put on the assassination list; and yet, as an American citizen, he was denied any of the Constitutional due process that all American citizens are entitled to. So, al-Awlaki was killed in an American drone attack in Yemen; several weeks later, his 16-year old son and another American citizen were killed in another drone attack. The Administration had to scramble to cover that up.

Now there are at least some indications that Anwar al-Awlaki may have been targeted for cold-blooded murder; because he was an FBI informant, and in that capacity, knew certain secrets about how this whole process and program of targeting was working, and perhaps knew of certain government ties to al-Qaeda. We don't know that, but there are court actions underway right now that may provide an even brighter light on the specific case of al-Awlaki.

FIGURE 3

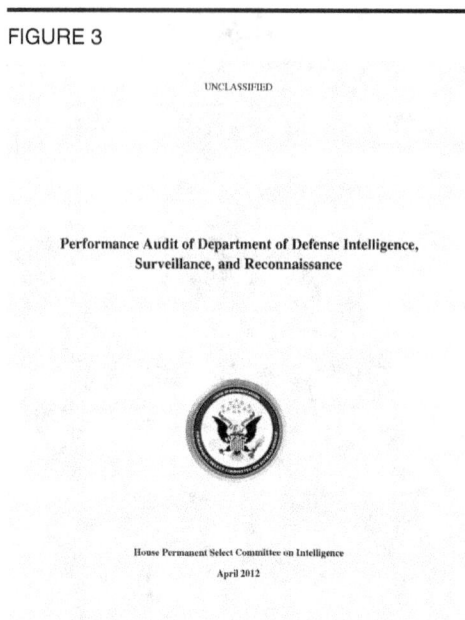

UNCLASSIFIED

Performance Audit of Department of Defense Intelligence, Surveillance, and Reconnaissance

House Permanent Select Committee on Intelligence
April 2012

This House Intelligence Committee report concluded that "the entire targetted-kill program was rife with violations, with failures to live up to any of the standards that would be appropraiate under the Constitution, or even under the Obama Administration's own guidelines."

Dept. of Defense/R.D. Ward
Gen. John Abizaid, former head of the Central Command, issued a report in 2014 noting "enormous uncertainties" in the drone program.

In Afghanistan, in Yemen, in Somalia, in Pakistan—those were the four major areas where this mass assassination campaign was taking place—there were extensive drone bases, massive amounts of military equipment. But yet, in all of the instances, it would appear that more often than not, the criteria that the Administration itself put forward were never in a single instance adhered to; and the collateral damage, the number of innocent people later, after the fact, posthumously declared enemy combatants was massive. We don't even begin to have a total death toll, but for every individual on the Presidential-approved kill list, there were multiple numbers of people who were killed simply because they were in the immediate vicinity.

One aspect of the program evolved to the point that targeted assassination operations were conducted on the basis of activity profile, not even identification of specific individuals. In the case of Afghanistan, there were instances where drone-targetted operations were directed against weddings, simply because the drones detected a large number of young males holding up guns in the air and firing them into the air. Now that happens to be part of a fairly typical tribal wedding ceremony in Afghanistan; so we don't know how many of these targeted assassinations were conducted on the basis of those kinds of activities.

Now, there was a report that was issued in 2014, that was done by General John Abizaid, who was the former head of the Central Command, and a lawyer from Georgetown named Rosa Brooks, who was a former attorney at the Department of Defense. And that report noted that there are "enormous uncertainties" in drone warfare, and that these uncertainties "are multiplied further when the United States relies on intelligence and other targeting information provided by a host nation government. How can we be sure we are not being drawn into a civil war; or being used to target the domestic political enemies of the host state leadership?"

So, in other words, this program was completely out of control, off the charts; but was thoroughly embraced by President Obama from his first days in office—probably initially courtesy of people like John Brennan. But the fact of the matter is that a massive number of crimes have been committed. The official documents, including those classified documents leaked out to *The Intercept*, make it clear that there was an absolute, unambiguous chain of command. In other words, the way that law enforcement would map out the structures of a mafia organization that they were going to break up; and unambiguously, the godfather of this entire mass kill program was President Obama. And if that doesn't constitute sufficient criteria for immediately launching impeachment proceedings or invoking of the 25th Amendment, then we've pretty much lost any sense of what our Constitutional republic is all about.

Doctors Without Borders

A destroyed area of the Doctors Without Borders hospital in Kunduz, Afghanistan, the morning after the U.S. bombing campaign.

Mayhem in Afghanistan

Ogden: OK, I would like to present the institutional question which we got in this week, which is very brief. It reads as follows: "Mr. LaRouche, the United States is to extend its military presence in Afghanistan beyond 2016. What is your opinion about the extension of our military presence in Afghanistan?"

Steinberg: Well, I think, first of all, you've got to consider the timing of this announcement. Regardless of whatever process there was, however long the deliberations were about making this decision, I find it extremely distasteful that the President chose to make this announcement just days after the United States had bombed the hospital of Doctors Without Borders in Kunduz.

There are new developments just in the last 24 hours, indicating that some American or NATO either tanks or APCs—armed personnel carriers—had arrived on the site soon after the bombing had ended, and had basically plowed through the rubble. And at least in the eyes of Doctors Without Borders, this was an attempt to bury and conceal evidence of a major crime that was committed. We spoke last week about the fact that Doctors without Borders had issued a call under the Geneva Convention for a top-down investigation, and they basically say that the actions that were undertaken under the auspices of President Obama, constituted war crimes.

So I think if you step back, and think about the thrust of what we've presented here in the last half hour or so, about the nature of the drone program, and then situate the bombing of this Doctors Without Borders hospital within that overall framework, I think you'll see that this situation is completely out of control, and lawless. In fact, one of the commentators who has been noting the horrors of this incident has pointed out that it may come down to the fact that President Obama's only legacy is that he will have been the only Nobel Peace Prize award recipient to bomb another Nobel Peace Prize recipient—because Doctors Without Borders has also been far more legitimately granted that award.

Your Musical Pathway from Dark Age Thinking to a Classical Renaissance

by Philip Ulanowsky

Oct. 19—The Presidential candidates' debate had begun; Having finished introductory remarks, the host now focused on the candidates. Tens of millions like you watched expectantly.

"Our first question tonight: How do you view the last half-century of cultural degeneration due to the rise and predominance of rock music, and, if elected, how do you propose to reverse it?"

Think twice before dismissing this fictional occurrence, and think carefully. Clearly, it bears no resemblance to any Presidential (or other government office) debate in the referenced half-century to date—though America has in its older experience, times when issues of similar cultural depth consumed the public interest. Today's serious citizen, of any persuasion, can find in the writings and speeches of inspiring earlier leaders in politics, science, and arts, language of conceptions born of an elevated mind, informed by the Classics. These were the ideas, presented to the public, upon which rested our greatest achievements in economic development, statecraft, scientific exploration, and technological advance.

Yet, who among those leading minds faced a global, civilizational moment as grave as ours? Who, despite the terrible ignorance and backwardness in many parts of the citizenry of their times, had to contend with a rock-music-brutalized population of several generations that would fight to defend its degeneracy, but not to free itself to participate in rescuing its own nation, descending from increasing illiteracy into a barbarism

Library of Congress

A Classical Standard: Abraham Lincoln delivers his Gettysburg address at the dedication of the National Cemetery there on Nov. 19, 1863.

proud of the depravity of its self-entertainment?

Rediscovering Beauty

To escape from the jaws of today's collapse, no mechanistic solution can succeed. The best program for economic revival must fail, unless we raise ourselves to wrestle with the uncomfortable reality that our own departure, over decades, from the truly creative in the sciences and arts alike, has "done us in." For various reasons, the most accessible pathway out of deadly, dark-age thinking for today's serious citizen, is a rediscovery of the beauty the Classical school of musical science presents to the mind.

In 1962, a leading Twentieth-Century Classical musician made some prescient remarks in his commencement address to an American conservatory's graduating music students. Accompanist Paul Ulanowsky (1908-1968), world renowned as a pianist, coach, and teacher, recalled his own youth in Austria, when "there was no TV then, of course; radio was not even in the crystal set stage; the record or rather phonograph industry concentrated on opera singers, with Caruso and Galli-Curci leading the field … and this, except for opera and public concerts, WAS IT. The music lover outside the larger cities therefore had to become a Do-it-yourself-addict, from sheer necessity." He followed this thought, referring to the increasing intrusions of instant electronic entertainment:

creative commons/Tomwsulcer

A Renaissance? txt me

If there is one thing which makes me nostalgic for that legendary state of affairs, it is that people used to put a different value on music. We live in a time and culture where its presence or absence is determined by the pushing of a button or the turning of a knob. It haunts and hounds us in restaurants and rest rooms, in elevators, stations, on trains and planes, in addition to other more conventional premises, at work and at leisure. This has inevitably led to a revision of the status of music in our civilisation and to a reappraisal which on occasion becomes agonizing in the truest sense of the word.

And this, decades before today's plague of ever-present personal listening devices had gripped an already increasingly asocial society. Could this process have contributed to your acceptance of today's degraded substitutes for your active participation in setting the nation's future course? Put it another way: What do you seek in your daily life that offers the quality of universal thought in which you may see reflected your own creative potential to grasp those vital conceptions needed to launch a new renaissance?

A Renaissance? txt me

As the seminal figures of Europe's Florentine Renaissance reached back to Ancient Greece for the ideas upon which to build a new society from the consequences continued from the Roman Empire's folly, so today we may look, also, to the highpoints of Western thought and culture before our present time. We will find the ideas we need in Classical musical science.

The perplexity of the very term "musical science" owes to the degeneration we must use great art to reverse. Leonardo da Vinci, the universal thinker, would have laughed at the question, "Which are you, a scientist or an artist?" The great Albert Einstein found the inspiration to overcome obstacles in his work by turning to his cherished violin; he was an accomplished Classical musician (as many of his leading predecessors had been). This was no escape to "feel good" music, no "easy listening" or "oldies favorites," let alone, of course, some guitar-smashing Dionysian abandon or mind-numbing repeated beat and rhythmic monotone rhyming. But, where, then, are "scientific ideas" in Classical music?

Admittedly, for the majority of today's public, *who have been robbed* of adequate opportunity to sing in a Classical chorus or perform in a similar instrumental ensemble, some introduction to the proverbial lay of the land is needed, something beyond the compass of this brief article—and far better discovered in a live, participatory setting. We can, however, say a few things here.

Where singing is involved, the Classical composers reflected, and often enhanced, the central irony of the chosen poem, Biblical text, or dramatic script (as in opera), by employing the various features of music to this end. These features are already known to everyone from ordinary speech.

You can, right now, conduct a little experiment, a musical one, to demonstrate your own knowledge of this, with this sentence. Read the sentence aloud, but remove the music from it—changes in pitch (keep your voice a dead monotone); in tempo (speed); in rhythm (different lengths of syllable or lengths of pauses between them); in accent (for instance, no accent on the second syllable of "experiment"); in tonal quality (harsh or soft, for example); in dynamics (loudness). Making sure to keep your voice unnaturally at exactly the same pitch throughout, you may enunciate either without any space in-between syllables (including between words) or with exactly the same length of break between all syllables, thus:

You-can-right-now-con-duct-a-lit-tle-ex-per-i-ment-a-mu-sic-al-one-to-de-mon-strate....

Becoming conscious of *how the music behind the words determines their meaning*, can be an important discovery in itself, and offers a window into the way a poem's or play's idea may be enhanced by adding one or more "voices" in the musical accompaniment to which it is set, an accompaniment that provides not merely a background to the words but an intimately interwoven feature of expressing the idea behind them. In some cases, changing the music of speech can impart the opposite meaning of the words themselves—an irony through "tone of voice." Coming to recognize and enjoy this interplay, however, is made difficult by addiction to virtually constant background music as entertainment, so easily pursued today.

In the same speech quoted above, Ulanowsky added something to his previous comment, after discussing the music teacher's role:

But there is something even more basic than exercise [of voice or instrument], something which is often overlooked in the pressures of a professional curriculum heavy with technique and literature. That is the meaning and value of Silence. Not just the measured silence of the rests between phrases and movements [of a piece], but that blessed primal silence which first created the need for sound.

This seems to me particularly essential at a time when we must compete in our music

From the author's personal collection

A Flemish harpsichord built in 1584 during the Flemish revolt against the Hapsburg empire. It is inscribed with the republican motto "Sine scientia ars nihil est." ("Without Science, Art is nothing.")

making with automobiles, dishwashers and other such gadgets. More than ever we must remind ourselves and others that music needs this inner silence and poise of listener and player alike.

Classical music, like a Shakespeare play, demands something of us to give forth its riches.

Where do we find ideas in music without singing, leaving us without words to guide our thoughts? Actually, music gains greater freedom to express universal 'scientific' ideas. Not, of course, if we accept the false prevalent, inculcated notion that scientific means mathematical or merely logical in the strict sense; instead, when science refers to discovery of provable principles of nature, including man, as the greatest scientists and artists (and, importantly, theologians) have understood it. As in communication in words or two-dimensional imagery, the language of music may present its own ironies—ambiguities or problems to be solved—and make its way to a resolution which the mind comprehends, just as the same mind may seek to resolve ambiguities and problems in science *per se* and other branches of knowledge. Art that is not merely "decorative," but enlivens and enriches the genuine creative faculties of artist and audience alike, serves the greater purpose of mankind in shaping the future.

The Gifts of Song

The composition, proper performance, and full appreciation of great music is not entirely easy, and indeed, much of the Classical musical singing literature reaches its pinnacle in the works of foreign composers—Mozart, Beethoven, Schubert, Verdi, and others—writing in languages other than English. Nonetheless, it is accessible and a pursuit which has formed a core of the LaRouche movement since its early days in the late 1960s, when Lyndon LaRouche, looking out at a sea of American college youth being seduced by a new fascist movement in the guise of "freedom" from Classical ideas, industry, and scientific progress, and "freedom" to sink into and spread existentialism and the rock-drug-sex counter-culture, determined, by himself, to create the germ of a new renaissance.

There is a rich record of Classical musical performance by those such as Ulanowsky and many others of his generation, whose intimate knowledge of, and passionate commitment to presenting faithfully, the ideas of some of the greatest minds in science and art, stands ready to inspire us. In such recorded performances, one may discover the striking difference between what we might call masterful storytelling, and the pathetic performance of a candidate repeating short phrases to incite animal calls from the audience. The difference between that which can rescue our humanity and that which defiles it.

To face the full reality of today's global collapse—the exciting positive developments of the BRICS and allied countries notwithstanding—requires a quality of personal courage needful of deep wellsprings and frequent refreshment. Classical music offers a personal emotional and intellectual connection to the great creative minds of the past, to the universal ideas they embraced, to the place in each of us where they resonate. The devaluation of the innate, uniquely human spark of divine creativity, the devaluation of human society which our youthful generations accept as simply normal, reaches each of us personally; the horrors in the daily news lie not merely outside ourselves as something we view as spectators at some sort of modern Roman Circus.

Within the works bequeathed us by the great Classi-

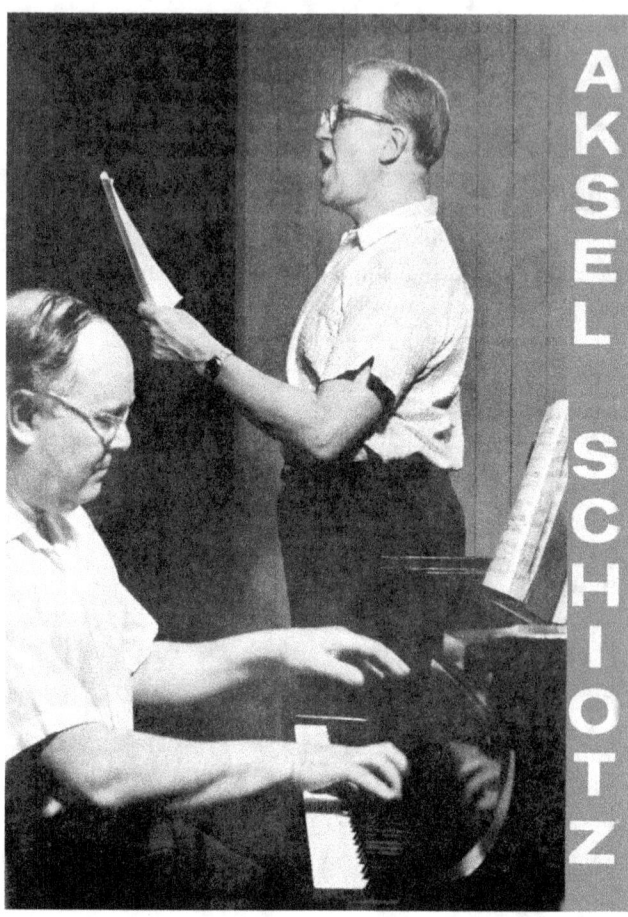

paul-ulanowsky.com

Paul Ulanowsky accompanying Danish tenor, and later bass, Aksel Schøtz in rehearsal for a Lieder album, after the singer's recovery from a stroke.

cal poets and composers, lies a treasure of beauty of a special kind, a kind in which we may find a reflection of that within ourselves which is most noble, from which to find the courage to change ourselves, to participate in the best of humanity, so that we may replace the rotting core of our dying nation with new spirit to attain the role America's founders wished for the republic so hard won from the brutish impositions of the British Empire then. As the great scientist Benjamin Franklin, emerging from the Constitutional Convention, answered to someone asking what kind of government had been created: "A republic, madam, if you can keep it."

If you wish to restore it today, don't look to a person or program from the outside, but to rejection of rock and its companions in irrationality, and relighting the lamp of Classical music, from within.

Philip Ulanowsky is the son of Paul Ulanowsky. More about the latter can be learned at the website paul-ulanowsky.org.

Manhattanites Raising Hell!

Here are edited excerpts from Lyndon LaRouche's Dialogue with the Manhattan Project on Oct 17, moderated by Dennis Speed.

Dennis Speed: Now, we're ready to go! My name is Dennis Speed, and on behalf of the LaRouche Political Action Committee, I want to welcome everybody here today. There's a lot that can be said, but there's a new conception, again, of the Manhattan Project, that Mr. LaRouche put forward. He's talked about the need to develop what he called a "Manhattan Party." I'm sure he'll be able to tell us exactly what he means by that. I'll just indicate, that after Mr. LaRouche opens, we'll go into our question and answer period, but we have a special presentation about something that we're going to do right after Lyn's opening remarks. So, Lyn, the floor is now yours.

Lyndon LaRouche: Okay, first of all, people will remember that we had a debate on Tuesday [Oct 13], it was an idiotic debate. [see *LaRouche: Democratic Debate Was a Fraud*, in this issue.] It was absolutely insane. Some of the people featured in that, on the stage, were sane; but most of the audience, in general, were a screaming bunch of idiots who had no understanding of anything. And at the same time, the way the thing was presented, as a campaign, was an abomination! There were some people in there who were not performing abominations, but the general effect was that the sponsor, Obama, was working on the basis of orders from a team in the British system. And that fraud was made as the Tuesday debate; it was a screwball debate which no sane person would willingly wish to do, unless they had some great duty to run, by going to the toilet or something, hmm!

But that's what happened. All the people who were running as candidates, or listed as candidates, were completely scrambled, or idiots, one of the two. Most of the best ones were scrambled, and the others were idiots. So this was an abomination beyond imagination, and the source of the thing was the British Empire which was directing Obama. That's what was happening. And that's the evil that we have to deal with today.

Now, in these premises, where many of us have met repeatedly among ourselves, and some people came in who weren't there before, and some people are not there who were before,—but that's a perfectly normal arrangement. But what we have to consider is this point, as in Manhattan in particular, which is usually our main point of departure for winning warfare. And for us, Manhattan is the center of all good things. That's doesn't mean that everything in Manhattan is good,—but it means the body itself has a good quality inside it, buried some place, or in some location.

Anyway, so this is what the issue is.

White House/Pete Souza

DNC Chairwoman Debbie Wasserman Schultz (right) was part of the set-up of the Democratic debate fraud. She was President Obama's personal choice. She's shown here with Obama (left), Interior Secretary Sally Jewell, and media "science guy" Bill Nye in Marine One, on Earth Day 2015.

Now, there've been people who've been operating, even some of our members of my organization, who have been sucked into playing games with the truth. And I have just announced to them that I would quit the organization if they tried to continue that—my organization! And I made it clear to the members attending a meeting earlier this day, that that would be the arrangement, and the people who were there,—all attending,—all agreed we would do that, that we had a couple of eightballs who got into our quarters and did some bad things.

So, we are now back on track, as we were, everything we did on Tuesday—what *we* did on Tuesday, not what they did on Tuesday, but what we did. And everything else. I think we are in a position to take charge. But we have to take charge, because we have a few people in our own organization who acted like clowns, and they have to be straightened out. But that will be fixed; I assure you, that will be fixed.

We had a meeting, of course, earlier this midday, and we settled everything. That is fixed. We are not going to go the way that Obama and his friends want us to go.

And so that's what the situation is. And I say this to this body here, which by its nature is a body of people who've met here with me many times now, so far, I thought we'd give you that straight confidence about what the situation is in general terms; and if you want some particular expression of that, I would be willing to deliver it, at least in an economical space of time.

So let's have some fun!

Speed: Yes, all right, let's go with the first report.

Taking on the Brits

Q: Hi Lyn, it's A— here. I'm going to talk to you about an intervention that took place yesterday, but it was Thursday afternoon that I was informed that there was an enemy sighting in Manhattan; and they were going to congregate at Peter Cooper Square, and some Baron, some fellow by the name of Adair Turner [Baron Turner of Ecchinswell] was going to talk about a book called *Debt and the Devil*.

And so this was a British operation that was going to take place. And there were four activists,—a member and three other activists that attended; I was there. The thing was attended by only about 32 people in a very large auditorium; it had a very low turnout, mostly Brits, a few Americans in there. And he spoke for about

an hour, and I swear to you it seemed like four. All mumble-jumble, the typical type of economics that you attack and ridicule.

So I thought it was clear to me what my job was to be, what my function should be there; and the interventions to break up the proceedings by just intervening and raising things like Glass-Steagall, Alexander Hamilton, and Abraham Lincoln, began about halfway into his presentation. One of the members was escorted out; I believe at that point they were still not aware that LaRouche PAC was present and in force there.

When the question-and-answer period came up,—you could hear people talking throughout, but I went to the mike, and I began by expressing to him that I was somewhat amused by his statements regarding economics and finance, when early in his remarks he had admitted that the crash of 2008 took him completely by surprise. Yet, he chose to come to the United States and tell us what financial policies he thinks we should be following.

But then I said: Actually, what I really want to raise is the austerity programs, or mission that you have, that policy, and that it really is about population reduction. And that his milieu of Sir Richard Attenborough, Prince Philip, and the President of the United States Obama, were all in line with this type of policy. And that's what your austerity and budget cuts really represented. Oh, I heard in the background, "How many more LaRoucheites are there in here! This is another LaRouche person!"

At that point, the heckling began for me to get to my question. And my question was as follows: "Why don't you, sir, take yourself and your crew, go back to England, find Cameron, and open a pig farm? Because you're all vermin."

They did not respond to that question.

Just before the proceedings began, we were informed that the former head of the Bank of England, Mervyn King, was sitting prominently in the front row. Now, what was interesting to me, was the smile that came up on my face when that happened, where frankly, not too long ago I would have been intimidated by such a thing. And indeed, in interventions that I was assigned to in the past, there were times when I just couldn't muster up,—the only thing that would elevate was my heart and my pulse,—but I couldn't get up and confront anybody on this. Yesterday was quite different: A smile came across my face, and then I knew even more so, what needed to be done.

So we ruffled some feathers. We disrupted their pretty little moment, and I think they know now that there are some people in New York that represent something, and we don't want any part of them.

LaRouche: I think that's most commendable and appropriate.

Defend the United States!

Q: Mr. LaRouche, this is R— from Bergen County, New Jersey. Last night, I was watching the webcast presented by Jeff Steinberg, and this to me was a complete bombshell. It's going to take a while to absorb everything; it was really quick in whatever time, an hour or so; and he brought out something that was released on Thursday, and if I could put it to the cameras, this is one of the articles that came out by Jeremy Scahill and Glenn Greenwald, [in *The Intercept*]—and there are actual military documents in this pack,—it was two in the morning and I printed out the whole thing. It's about 300 pages long, and I've started reading it.

This thing is absolute dynamite, as far as I'm concerned. The subtitle is "Secret military documents expose the inner workings of Obama's drone wars.'" And Jeff last night mentioned this: that every President since Gerald Ford has upheld an executive order banning assassinations by U.S. personnel. "Congress has avoided legislating the issue or even defining the word 'assassination.' This has allowed proponents of the drone wars to rebrand assassinations with more palatable characterizations, such as the term du jour, 'targeted killings.'" And I know that you have mentioned this many times over the past number of years.

I think we've implicitly, at least I have implicitly, known about this from other sources, about the Tuesday meetings where decisions are made, but the thing that differentiates this documentation is that there are specific government documents that have been obtained which nobody can ignore—*nobody* can ignore what's

The Drone Paper released Oct. 15 by Glenn Greenwald's The Intercept have put vivid, documented evidence of Obama's record as a mass murderer on Congress's doorstep for action.

written here.

And this is a shredding of the Constitution, completely and totally. It's been going on probably since the beginning of the Bush Administration, through now; Congress seems to be doing absolutely nothing about this issue. It's a flagrant violation of the Constitution; it's a flagrant violation of international law; there's all kinds of war crimes affiliated with this; this is not only about particular "terrorists" being targetted and killed, regardless of their nationality and situation. Anyone who is in the near vicinity of somebody who is targetted, is considered to be a terrorist as well, so the killing of individuals, "collateral damage" so to speak, has no credence whatsoever.

So what's my point on this? To me this is a huge incentive to get this out to Congress. I mean, it's going to do one of two things: Either Congress is going to do something about it, which has to lead to impeachment. There's no way one can look at these documents and go into an investigation of this, without bringing up the issue of impeachment. *It has to come up.* Now, if Congress ignores it, what does that say about Congress? They're criminals! They're total criminals if they ignore it.

So I love what Jeff brought out, and I think this thing is great. And I know I have started badgering my Congressman about it, but I'd appreciate any comments you might have.

LaRouche: Well first of all, we had an event which followed the Tuesday so-called debate. Now this was ordered by, specifically, Obama. But Obama, to my knowledge since early last Friday,—was merely a stooge for a British invasion into the affairs of the United States, and the British interests were the people that were specifically supporting Obama in this policy.

Now my view of that point is, severally, first of all, the whole thing, the whole show of that Tuesday debate was a sideshow, one of the most corrupt things ever presented in modern times by any part of the United States government. This was the most evil thing ever generated in the recent centuries of the United States. This was *treason* in the worst extreme. And Obama was the prime embodiment of that.

Now, on the specific case that you did make reference to, in particular, in this case, we have Jeff Steinberg together with two other people on our team, who on Friday evening presented a summation of the most essential facts about this whole matter. And I had identified the British angle on the Friday before the debate there, and I had the picture. Then, we did on this recent Friday, we had the whole fact laid out by three people in our webcast [see *Obama Indicted* in this issue] at eight o'clock yesterday; the whole structure, including what Jeff Steinberg did at some length, was supplied at that point.

It's also clear that certain people inside my own organization have played opportunist games with reality. And I told them that either I throw them out, or they throw me out. And I think the people who met today, on Saturday, who are leading people in our organization there, all concurred with that estimation. So what we're doing is, we're going to clean house, in our way: We're going to defend the United States! We're going to drive the British invaders out of our existence, and we're going to bring members of our Congress into conformity with the purposes of our Constitution. And that's the approach we will take. And I will be absolutely merciless on this issue, on that point. Anybody who's going to try to destroy and corrupt the United States while I'm still alive, is going to have a big problem.

And if I happen to die in the meantime, it's still going to be a rather big problem for them. Because my corpse will stink all over the place on them.

So let's fight! Have fun!

A Concept of Immortality

Q: Hi Lyn, it's M—. I wanted to get your thoughts on something that had come up. Rachel Brinkley and I had gone to an event here in the city earlier this week, to intervene. The event was on the subject of the "Resistance against Injustice." The speakers were Cornel West and Chris Hedges, and to give you a kind of a characterization of it: It was a dialogue; the whole thing was the two of them onstage speaking to each other; there were about 150 people in the room, most of whom were associated with different leftist groups, with their issues and such. And they were discussing the character of someone in the fight.

So West, who's a civil rights leader, was talking about questions of striving for virtue. He discussed the idea of learning to die before you can learn to live, but you have to get over your fear of death, and then you can fight. But he said, "I'm not optimistic, but I have hope." [LaRouche chuckles]

Hedges had a different take. Hedges has written whole books on the resistance fight, and has an interesting background. He was working at the *New York Times* for fifteen years, but resigned when he refused to cave in to pressure to stop speaking out against the Iraq War. However, what he was focussed on for this discussion was to communicate to the audience that you have to resist, but you have to do so knowing that you will never succeed. [laughter] He said, "the enemy is too big and powerful; you will fail." He said, "everything you do in the grand scheme of things is futile, but it is not meaningless."

So we intervened during the forum, of course, and they agreed on the issues *per se*: impeaching Obama, Glass-Steagall; but I spoke to Hedges afterwards; they had both referenced Kant. So what I brought up to Hedges was, "Have you ever read Schiller?" And he said he hadn't, and I briefed him a little bit on Schiller taking on the failure of the Enlightenment, that you had this enlightened class who failed to achieve the political victory. The French Revolution was a failure. And that Schiller was intervening to address, to fix the moral failures of the educated class, so that we could succeed and uplift mankind. So he expressed some interest in reading Schiller, but then said, "To be honest, I'm a Calvinist, and don't have a very high view of mankind."

So my concern was, what's the effect on the audience in having their leaders tell them "you can't expect to succeed?" So I wanted to get your thoughts on this problem.

LaRouche: The answer is very simple. If they have that problem, they're not thinking, [laughs] they're disqualified as leaders. If they're this weak-brained, weak-minded thing, it's impossible. Yes. There are a lot of people like that. And they rotate around; you used to find them around Harvard University, similar places like that; they would gather around in the streets. I had a lot of experience with that stuff, so I refer to it for that reason. But it was crap. Plainly. And they were gutless wonders.

The question is, what are you going to do for the

"A man who won't die for something is not fit to live," said Rev. Martin Luther King. Here he's shown addressing the Aug. 28, 1963 March on Washington.

future of mankind? Everyone dies. Every human being dies,—it is inevitable. Now, sometimes people are more fortunate in having a longer life; sometimes it's a worse alternative in their mind.

So therefore, the question is, how do we organize people to respond to the fact, that while all people die, all human beings die, nobody but a human being has a concept of immortality of mankind, which only mankind has. In other words, when you die, if your life is useful in creating the future, as an advancement in the future, your life was not wasted. This is something that soldiers in warfare, in general warfare, have had to deal with, and they've dealt with it. Many soldiers of the United States, both in the war before mine, and my war, and the war that followed, these were tough wars. A lot of people died. A lot of my friends died. Some didn't die. A lot of friends suffered from the effects of the forces which took over the United States when Franklin Roosevelt had died.

And ever since Franklin Roosevelt had died, we've been fighting against the Wall Street crowd most intently. Wall Street was looking for vengeance against Franklin Roosevelt! It's a Satanic force! Frankly you have to say, it's a Satanic force. *Wall Street is a Satanic force.* The British Empire is a Satanic force. There are other things.

But let's look at chiefly,—there are also options. There are nations, and populations in nations, who really are honest and who work. The increase of the productive powers of labor is actually a moral proposal, rather than just something to be admired. It's a necessity. And therefore, the creative powers of mankind, that is, the ability of the dead person to have, in advance, have created an advancement to the benefit of the life of humanity in general... That is the purpose of human life: is to perpetuate the progress of mankind by expending one's life in the purpose of creating a better future for mankind as a whole, in the course of living.

And so all these kinds of things of how you deduce things, and can compare things, and so forth—it's really nonsense. The question is, what is the sum total of what a nation can contribute to humanity, or what the individual person, by living, can contribute to humanity? These are the real moral issues. This includes the extension to space, to the Galaxy, to Kepler. These are foreign things, in foreign areas. We have planets within the Solar System and beyond, which will sooner or later be mastered and made use of by mankind from Earth.

It is mankind's contribution to the universe, to the extent that mankind *has* a contribution, to give and is able to give, to the universe, as such. And, that's mankind's intention; that's mankind's purpose in existing: Is the ability to create the elimination of evil, and of waste of time—which is an evil—the waste of life, of not responding to the opportunity of making the condition of humanity better. So, the idea of the making humanity better for all people, as possible, is the primary concern, and the proper devotion of every sane, developed personality. [applause]

Fighting for the Human Species

Q: Good afternoon, Lyn. It's B— from New Jersey. Although I did want to point out that given the amount of events that we've had going on in Manhattan, I consider myself at least a New York City strap-hanger. [laughter]

In any case, I did want to report on another event that occurred yesterday over in New Jersey at Rutgers University, which was sponsored by the New Jersey Citizen's Action Coalition. The main theme of the event was that they brought people in to identify areas where, in effect,—people were saying,—people are being put under economic slavery, and numerous people at the event brought that out, whether it was the occurrence of pay-day loans, student loans, the fact of people losing their houses.

In fact, yesterday morning, when I opened my local paper, there was an article where the State of New Jersey is now getting $300 million of revenue this year from the sale, by the towns in the state, of tax liens. In other words, investors come in, they buy up the tax liens, where people can't afford to pay the taxes on their houses, and these investors turn around and can get anywhere up to 18% interest against the taxes that people can't afford to pay in the first place.

So, that was basically the theme. At the end of the first panel of the event, Rachel Brinkley, who had gone there with me, and another person, brought up in the first question, the issue of Glass-Steagall, and of the continued financial collapse, and that's what these people were really talking about. And that seemed to, from that point on, change the entire dynamic,—from people bringing up, in the next panel, the fact that Elizabeth Warren had gone to school there, and was now down in Washington, D.C.,—although people generally associate her being from Massachusetts, that she'd actually been taught there, and was now in Congress, fighting for Glass-Steagall.

One of the first speakers was a Senator from here in New Jersey who has not signed on yet, but who had been approached by myself and others on Glass-Steagall. The next speaker was a Congressman from New Jersey, who in fact on the previous Wednesday, I'd been able to talk to, when our delegation intervened down in Washington, D.C.

So, immediately, that's what everybody started talking about. Either that, or there were already people there who knew what Glass-Steagall was about. The former Speaker of the New Jersey Assembly was there, who is a co-sponsor of the Glass-Steagall resolution in the New Jersey Assembly. I had a chance to talk to her and another person outside, who turned out to be the president of the County Freeholders, and when I approached them, she turned to this person and said, "Here's my guy on Glass-Steagall,"—because I'd spoken, over the period, to different people in the Assembly and Senate on Glass-Steagall. So, it's very well-known. In fact, the only signer on Glass-Steagall down in Washington from the New Jersey congressional delegation, was a former New Jersey Assemblyman and sponsor of the Glass-Steagall resolution there.

So, that's what everybody started talking about. And, unlike the previous report that Michelle gave, what started to happen was we started motivating people on Glass-Steagall. There was a lady from the NAACP who took resolutions to get signed, to turn over to her local congressman—in fact, the same congressman that I just referenced, who is not signed on down there. We had other people doing the same thing. They wanted us to get back to them. The President of the Freeholders said, "I want a sit-down meeting with you. We have to discuss this issue of Glass-Steagall."

I'm hoping that, because there are a lot of events going on, that you, and others, are getting a lot of these reports on, in fact, a level of activity that is going on, and has been going on, particularly in the last couple of weeks. Anyway, I did want to bring that out to you, and I hope people will pass on to you a lot of these reports.

LaRouche: They are coming, these reports, and I'm making some of these reports myself, eagerly, in order to get this thing in the shape needed. We have to get rid of Obama. It's understandable. Obama must be ejected from office *now*. It's an urgent matter. The very continued existence of the United States depends upon removing Obama from office now. Because Obama has never been anything except a stepson of one of the most murderous, mass-murderous, people in life.

In other words, his stepfather was the most evil man of his time, that we know of. But the stepfather allowed his mother—that is, Obama's mother—to get out of that particular area,—but what happened was, the effect was that Obama inherited the disease which was the characteristic of his stepfather. He was one of the worst murderers in that whole region, and Obama is an heir of that habit. Obama is an evil man, who should not have been brought into any public office of authority.

Now we've had him, in our case, for two terms now. We also had Bush. Now the second Bush was a wimping, stupid idiot. But there was Dick Cheney. Cheney made up for the lack of evil found in the poor dumb Bush. He really was a Bush-league character; the kind that couldn't set fire. But that's what he was.

So, this is what we've been suffering with. We got now four terms of two U.S. Presidents. And these four terms of two U.S. Presidents have been a force of evil against the people of the United States! Bush, twice. Cheney, involved. And also Obama. Obama is evil, pure evil, everything about him.

Now, we published last night a report which included that of two of my particular associates, in the webcast we broadcast last night. And some of that information is circulating through other channels now. We're circulating it, actually, heavily. We're laying down some heavy evidence. And we're also correcting people who become stupid once in a while; we don't like to have our people become stupid. We consider that a liability to their achievements.

But that's the point. We're in that kind of situation. We're in a fighting situation. And, we're fighting for something, not fighting for a cause, but fighting for the defense of the continuation and promotion of the human species, which is the only thing really worth fighting for. It's the proper devotion of success for any individual, any human individual: is to have the ability and resources to make a contribution to the future of mankind, which is systemic, not just particular. And, that's the thing we must always fight for—fight for the improvement of the moral and intellectual qualities of the human individual, especially on a large basis.

\ creative commons/Bxsstudent

The Bronx High School of Science, one of the institutions of relative educational excellence in the Manhattan area.

Q: Good afternoon, Mr. LaRouche. Hi!
LaRouche: Oh! My good old friend!

The Einstein Model

Q: [follow-up] Yea. [laughing] This is E—, from the Bronx. I would like to ask you,— you stress that there is no creativity in mathematics. But what about the men that invented the mathematics that we have today? Like algebra, geometry, trigonometry, calculus. Weren't they being creative? Weren't they finding out discoveries in those fields of mathematics? They created those fields of study. And suppose there would be a mathematician today who would invent the new branch of mathematics, called under a new name, like geometry was a new branch to algebra. Trigonometry was a new branch. Calculus was a new branch. Wouldn't that be creative, in a sense?

LaRouche: All those things you listed, are things I despise! [laughs]

Q: [follow-up] Say that again, please?

LaRouche: Because they are all wrong! What had happened, the period of competent science—and there was only one outstanding scientist in the Twentieth Century. Only one, and he was Jewish. [laughs]

Q: [follow-up] Einstein?
LaRouche: Einstein. Albert Einstein was the only competent scientist in the Twentieth Century. The others were make-ups. Einstein was the greatest intellectual figure in science in the Twentieth Century. All the others were imitations, or cheap-skates, or cheap-shots. So the problem today is: mathematics has become, as it's been taught in the Twentieth Century, and now presently is even worse—mathematics as taught is the destruction of the mental powers of the human individual! And the greatness of mathematical work died out, except for Einstein and a few other people like him, associated with him; and I knew a couple of those individuals, and I worked with them, who were not insane, who were not rotten, who were successful, who were great.

But what we've had in the schools,—well, we have some teachers who are very serious and very sincere, and the work they did is,—according to the standard which was given to them,—they were excellent in terms of their accomplishments as teachers.

Particularly the Manhattan area, in teachers, had one of the best standards for education, in public education. It was because Manhattan was an area in which poor people, coming into New York City and surviving there, or around New York City, were able to develop culture and life as something meaningful.

Most other parts of the United States were deprived, especially the Southern States. The Southern States are really not civilized. Some people like to be civilized, but they aren't really qualified to be civilized. So therefore, we've had a destruction, a *progressive* destruction overall, over the Twentieth Century, and into now the present Twenty-first Century. That has been a period of increasing

The living standards of the American black population as a whole reflect the "systematic intention to eliminate them," said LaRouche.

degeneration of the minds and science of the human population. The issue now, which is one we should hold for a consideration in Manhattan, in particular,—we should take over the effecting of a change, which follows the precedent of Albert Einstein, and use him as a model of reference for progress. Once you have that standard clearly in your mind, you understand what was wrong with the rest of the people.

Speed: That's a really good idea.

Q: Good afternoon Lyn, this is your 95-year-old World War II veteran, B—, back here at you again. [Applause.]

LaRouche: Well, I'm only 93 years old. You're my senior.

Q: [follow-up] I'm doing fairly well, Lyn, all things considered. Bruce Todd and I went this past Wednesday down to visit our Congressman at his office. Of course he was absent, but his secretary took down everything that we had to say to him; and she's going to get back to us, and we'll be looking forward to her getting back to us. Our next endeavor will be to visit a Senator, and bring to his attention about the Glass Steagall, which neither one of them have actually signed onto yet. So we'll be clobbering them and doing anything else we can, outside of breaking a leg. Just want to let you know, sir, we're working on it diligently. Have a good afternoon.

LaRouche: [laughs] Thank very much. Good to talk to you again.

Wall Street vs. Black Americans

Q: Good afternoon, Mr. LaRouche, how are you?
LaRouche: I'm alive.

Q: [follow-up] Good to see you. I'm E—. I'm actually visiting from Alabama, I came up here last week for the 20th anniversary of the Million Man March, which of course you had something to do with putting together.

Of the things that happened as a result of this 20th anniversary commemoration, is, Robert Kennedy Jr. sent a message to everybody who participated in the march in relationship to vaccines. That's because he's working with a whistleblower from the CDC, who discovered that some data had been covered up, or communicated in the wrong manner, that covered up information to the effect that black boys who received certain vaccines were having very high rates of autism; but the reports covered up that fact, so we're only now discovering this.

And this follows, of course, maybe a 40 or 50-year increase in the rates of autism, and people trying to figure out why those rates are increasing. And one of the theories for many years has been that maybe vaccines are part of that, particularly the kind of preservatives they put in vaccines; they put mercury in, they put aluminum in, which are heavy metals which are toxic to the brain.

However, the medical establishment recently said, well, no, vaccines are not a cause of autism. But since then, this whistleblower came up with this new information, and he tried to bring the information to the black leadership, but nobody would listen to him; I'm talking about Robert Kennedy now. And he finally brought it to Minister Farrakhan, and Minister Farrakhan is sharing that information with everyone, and has called for a march on the CDC on Oct. 25th, which is this week coming up. So, I just wanted to share that information, and see what thoughts you may have on that. Thank you.

LaRouche: The problem with something what occurred—I don't know the full facts of that. I do know, because at my age I do not follow some of the things I would have earlier,—but, the point is, the case is plausible, in fact, but it also is consistent with the effect on the population: that the so-called black population has actually been selectively targeted in a way which was not experienced in earlier times, that is relatively earlier modern times, say Twentieth Century times. There's nothing like that; which I know it's a fact it's occurring. I know the phenomena, the evidence of the effect of the phenomena. I do not have a direct knowledge of what the information might be.

But I say if it's not some kind of drug, it's something in terms of behavior consideration, or the use of drugs, which is abundant in the population. That's the problem; being driven into drug-*using* itself would have an effect like that, if there's something that juices that up with some direct poison.

But I think of certain smoking habits, certain drug habits which become common among youth who are desperate. And that has been increasing during whole parts of the Twentieth Century. The first part of the Twentieth Century was less evil in this question, but it was during the second part of the century, where things began to really get evil.

And it came together coincident with poverty. It came directly to specifically, Negro quality of persecution. All these things are true.

As I say, I don't know the exact mechanism that occurred in any particular case. But I do recognize a causal factor in the educational system, the living standard of people in terms of the black population; there is absolutely a very systematic intention to eliminate them, in effect. If you take the trend line, and you take the second half of the Twentieth Century, and you then go into the present phase of the subsequent century, you see this is an abundant characteristic of the nation.

And therefore, this has to be attended to on that basis. And instead of trying to pick one thing as a factor, why not pick out the factor as a whole? Why don't we

stop what has happened to the black population in these areas? And particularly the killing rates,—they're astonishing!

And, yes, this is an issue which must be attended to in a systematic way. I don't think I know any one cause, except the policy of Wall Street, and the policy of Wall Street is the suitable account for this effect.

Speed: I'll just indicate also there's a nine-minute tape, Lyn, that we'll make sure to get you, which was sent out by Robert Kennedy Jr., which just sort of goes through his particular take. He makes clear he's not anti-vaccine; he's talking about a very specific vaccine.

That's not in response to what you just said, I just wanted to let people know that exists.

Formula for Lifting Up Nations

Q: Good afternoon, sir. My name is S—M—from Tuskegee, Alabama, and I'm just listening, I'm absorbing, and you're very stimulating, and I have a ton of reports that I would like to share, but I'm aware of the economy of time.

So in recognition of that, I do feel the need to start out by acknowledging and thanking you, and those who labor with you, for the work you did in the birthing of the original Million Man March. That made a lot of things possible for me as a young black man. I worked organizing on the Million Man March, and had the pleasure of meeting and working with Rev. James Bevel in our association with the Million Man March.

That being said, I'm here actually by way of the Million Man March I attended last week, and I think it would be important for you to know that in my community, we had a generation of crack babies that made it to the Million Man March. They were there; these are people, they really were crack babies, with *everything* that that means attached to it. And I labored this year to reconnect them to unsponsored leadership, i.e., Minister Farrakhan was successful *without* media. This was done through social media, this was done through radio. We had no media coverage. BET [Black Entertainment Television] had an award, where guys were singing about the love of cocaine and baking soda. So, you know, this was happening while we were gathering in D.C. The youth, the Native Americans, the Latinos, the women, were very encouraged by the fact that we did this without the media. So now there's another whole avenue open for us and things to discuss.

Now, in 2001, we had 666 murders in Chicago, and

Atonement Memorial Garden

Press Conference
10:00 a.m.
Blue Seas Restaurant
205 W MLK Hwy
Tuskegee, AL 26083

Groundbreaking
11:00 a.m.
Fonville mini-farm
Fonville & Rosa Parks
(next to Club Extreme)
Tuskegee, AL 36083

Celebration of Life

Students for Education and Economic Development (SEED Inc) is building our first Atonement Memorial Garden in Tuskegee in memoriam of four young men murdered in the city as an atonement for allowing our community to arrive to this point.

We are working with the families of the victims, university student organizations, the police and sheriff departments, city and county leadership, and the community at large in designing a beautiful edible park which will house the Atonement Memorial Garden.

On Saturday, September 26, 2015, we will be holding a press conference to announce our plans. The press conference will be followed by a groundbreaking ceremony and a demonstration of the bio-intensive method of organic farming that will be used in the 1.4-acre mini-farm.

The advertisement for the press conference held by Students for Education and Economic Development (SEED, Inc.) on Sept. 26, to announce the memorial for four young men murdered in Tuskegee, Alabama.

out of the 666, 538 were black; it was 430 males and 78 females; and then 112 were Mexican; and the rest were filtered between others.

I designed a project for Reverend Bevel called the War on Murder. He said he wanted it, and just when we were about to launch it, well, a big mess hit—not unrelated to what we were doing in Chicago, I might add. And if I ever have an opportunity to share with you what I experienced, I would like to do that.

However, even after the mess, we never stopped our work, and we have been setting up chapters to launch this war effectively around the country. And Sept. 26th in Tuskegee, we launched a model of this War on Murder. We took a memorial I would call an Atonement Memorial Garden; we designed edible parks in these neighborhoods; we bring the people to help us grow the edible parks, and we designed Atonement Memorial Gardens to memorialize the victims of murder. We brought the mothers out, we brought the families out.

Something that is very, very, very important to realize: When we go to memorialize these boys and girls who were murdered, these are the ones that everybody forgets about or throws to the side. When I go to memorialize Tyrone, all his friends show up. They were waiting for us in the park. The ones nobody can talk to, the ones nobody can seem to get to come to any functions like this, where good information is happening. When I got to the park, they were waiting; and we began reintroducing people to one another.

We began to have the mothers tell stories about their children, and why they were loved, because when we were researching the murders in the newspapers, you get a paragraph, and it said, well, this one was involved with marijuana, or this one had a gun, or whatever, but nobody said this was a living soul created in the image and likeness of God, and had he had what he needed, this could not have occurred.

So that is part of the work that we're doing. We had a very successful groundbreaking. We called it the "War on Two Fronts." My front is what is going on in the neighborhoods—us killing us. That's my front. I don't get off into a lot of what the police are doing or what others are doing. I have to start with what we're doing, because if we want justice, we have to agree to be the source of justice.

So the mothers had to get up, and the qualifications for speaking was to speak to what my contribution to the murder of my loved one is. And that's what the whole of that meeting looked like. And so it elevated the energy resonance and the facility, and it spilled over, and it began bringing people who were just passing by into the meeting with us.

So it was very successful. I really cannot do this report justice. I need for you to be able to hear exactly what we're doing, and a response as you formulate how you would like to move forward against the forces that are arrayed against us as a whole, I would like you to know some of the tools that you would have at your disposal. And at that I would like your response. Thank you.

LaRouche: Thank you. Well, on this matter, I think the issue is that we have to actually, rather than going at the details—the details are very important, the details that you dealt with—that's an aspect of the whole problem of our nation. And it has to be treated in the proper place, in the proper way. We have to deliver results. And we have to concentrate on the results that are necessary in that particular case, because that case is a major problem, for many reasons in the United States as a whole. For historic reasons, the history of the Confederacy, all of these kinds of things all go together in one thing.

And therefore, what we need is a coherent, complete approach to what the needs are of this nation and of the world, and both are inseparable. This nation and the world are inseparable issues, and we have to find the formula to solve those problems.

For example, you've got the case of what Putin is doing, in Russia and outside of Russia. That is an example of a curative measure among nations. What China is doing today is a beautiful example of the accomplishment of nations rising from a relatively backward area, into a great spurt of achievement. The same thing is happening in India. Now India is a place I've had much dealing with in the course of my life, and yes, they are also improving.

And what we're trying to do is to bring the system of nations into a new kind of coherence, not one of each one nation at a time, but the way in which we can integrate, the struggle of nations for development of the quality of the human mind for all people. And we have the mechanism, especially in Russia—it's there. It's a damaged nation; Russia is a damaged nation, but it's been reconstructed under the leadership of Putin. We have other nations, which are struggling with the same thing. China is really a wonderful achievement. India will become more and more an achievement. We have other parts of the world. We have people in South America, nations of South America which are trying to struggle their way through to the kind of authority which they justify to get rid of the British and the U.S. actually ruining these nations. The nations are being ruined. But we can fight for that; we can fight against that sort of stuff.

And the time has come that we have to take a human, a worldwide and beyond, *human* approach to the subject of mankind. Because mankind is the only creature, the only living creature which is capable of mastering the Galaxy, or mastering what Kepler did. You have to be able to go into not only the Solar System, but beyond the Solar System, as Kepler demonstrated for the first time. Now the Galactic studies now, are giving you another lesson. Mankind has a destiny to increase mankind's abilities, in order to reach control of Mars, to reach control of the Galactic System, too. And on that basis we find that mankind has a destiny, which is unique to mankind, to reach out and to move the stars. And if we take that view and that approach, we will not miss any of the essential accomplishments.

Set the Standard for Justice

Q: Hello, my name is R— M— and I was invited here. This is my first time, and there are two topics I really want to discuss. One is the failing public school system, with Mayor De Blasio putting four high schools in one school; 30 kids to a classroom: How could a teacher teach that? People are out to line their own pockets. The kids are being taught to a test; they're not actually learning anything.

The minority kids are failing between the cracks in the public school system. Not only that, you got 90% of the minority, colored folks, Hispanics,—they're living in shelters, transitional homes,—but they have all these zombie buildings, empty, abandoned buildings that have been around for years. Why can't you fix them up and open them up and make them for schools, and for housing for people to have somewhere to live?

They're pricing seniors out of their homes. If you don't have good health insurance you don't get the proper service in the hospitals. I mean the economy, what Obama, Mayor De Blasio, and all them are doing, is really wrong! What is your opinion on this?

LaRouche: Well I think we could say some things on that point. The point is, first of all, mankind has the capabilities which only mankind has. Mankind is not classifiable as an animal. Mankind cannot be an animal. Some people will behave like animals, but that's because they're misbehaving. And I say misbehaving in the literal meaning of that term.

So therefore, what are we up to? We are up to coming to create a change in the destiny of mankind. This process is already in process in China. It's brought back into process in India; it's being pushed by Putin in Russia and around there and so forth. So we have all these cases of a tendency to achieve a new status of mankind. Now the idea of this new status of mankind is already a good idea, but we need to be more specific about it. And we mean to have a redefinition of what education is, among other things; and for the circumstances under which people live and work and so forth. So we need that. We will not be able to succeed, if we limited ourselves to picking on certain issues.

We have to have a broad issue, which is applied to the population as a whole, and the point is, how do we develop the child? How do we educate the child? How many people talk about that today? How many people really understand what that problem is? Then we get beyond to the school grades, and you find the rate of degeneration, of the intellectual character of the stu-

WANG Hongying/CC BY

Chinese students at a special summer camp set up on Luxi Island, a remote island off the coast.

dents coming out since that period, the Twentieth Century—the scheme has been generally downward. The quality of life is downward.

What do you have in the United States today? We have a bunch of very, very poor people—extremely poor people; people without opportunities, with no future. You can't say that one category of person is the limit; you have to say there has to be a broad, universal standard of progress, for *all*, because if you weaken one, you weaken them all by that margin.

And what we have to do now is realize we have an enemy. The enemy is called Obama. He is Obama. He's a Satanic figure, whose stepfather was a mass killer and the current President Obama is a mass killer. That's on the record. He's systemically a mass killer, and a thief and everything else.

It's a broad issue. We have to say, "What is the standard which we, as leaders in society, that is, leaders in terms of education, and knowledge, experience,"—we have to force the issue *now*. We have all these people that are being killed in Europe, *killed*. In other places as well; killed off. So we've got to get a concept of justice, and the intention for the purpose of mankind's further existence, has to be supplied. I think we can do that. And I think that this city, *this city* which is the keystone city of the United States, as Alexander Hamilton made clear, and he's still right. And if we take that point of view and say we're going to organize the United States, as the first target of responsibility

for us... We've got to go upward, for a change.

And what you're talking about, yes, there's one way that can work. We have to have a wide, broad, inclusive area; support the development of the children of all families. And we have to make sure the education of the children, actually increases, their power to create, not how to behave, but to create!

Look to the Galaxy

Q: Good afternoon, Mr. LaRouche. This is S— from Manhattan. My question is about the South China Sea. Just a couple of days ago, China announced, as a counter to the U.S. wanting to go over to the South China Sea to keep them in check, they offered the surrounding nations to do joint military drills with them. So if the U.S. does go over there, it's going to stick out like a sore thumb that they're not trying to contain China, they're trying to contain the entire region. So I would like to know the strategic importance of China offering to do joint military drills with the rest of the surrounding countries?

LaRouche: Well, China has taken a very shrewd approach to this matter. And you know, China is a nation with a certain history, and people of China will tend to echo significant parts of China's history. And they will concentrate on leading forces in China who are more suitable to effect the progress of the people of China.

And therefore the Chinese government does not necessarily react in the way in which Obama wants them to react. And if they get too nasty, China and other forces will do something about it. India will do something about it. Russia will do something about it. A few nations in Africa will do something about it, those that have some independence, and relatively more strength; they will do something about it. People in South America will do something about it, and so forth.

So therefore, the point is the creation of a unity, of commitment to realize that we have to deal with the human species as a species. We're not looking at who's to be the guys to be cut off and who's to be promoted. The issue is, what has to be promoted? It's the human species.

A Chinese fishery administration ship, background, guards a Chinese fishing vessel in December 2014 near the disputed Spratly islands in the South China Sea—an area of intense provocation by the Obama Administration.

And when you think about what Kepler has accomplished in the first important treatment of this very subject-matter; and then you look at the Galactic process as such, look at what that involves. What is this? This is mankind in motion to change the Galaxy, or the one Galaxy. And one good galaxy achieved, might lead to a next good galaxy to be added to that. That's where mankind is going. That's where the direction is, in which mankind's destiny and educational process must go! We must create our role in contributing to the system! The stellar system.

And mankind can do it. Look, the idea of the Martian colonization. Well, you could develop something which is human on Mars. That's going to be a very tough thing to deal with. *But!* Mankind has the means of access to Mars. Not to live there, but to develop Mars, and to develop improvements on Mars which will benefits other parts of the Solar System and beyond.

So we have to change the subject, from the usual gob-gob-gob, whatever thing they do,— forget it! We have to say, what is mankind? as Nicholas of Cusa said, what is mankind? for example. Therefore, you have Christian leaders, like Nicholas of Cusa and other persons associated with him. Leibniz, for example, similar, universal people. Leibniz spent time in developing China, in a period of his life. When you get a person like Leibniz, and you take the history of Leibniz, you find

there a more appropriate, approximate example, than any other location. What Leibniz accomplished in his lifetime, is an example of what the human species can accomplish, because that was what Leibniz was working on.

Q: Hi, Mr. LaRouche, my name is R— from New York City. I first became aware of your intellect back in 2006, when I read your very prescient prediction that real estate was going to collapse. I was living in Middleburg [Virginia] and Atoka Chase, and you're in Leesburg. And I think along the way, you talked about creating a water infrastructure in the United States. Critical to human survival and the advancement of the species, it appears, would be the abundance of clean water, and California's having a huge problem; so are many of the states in the West. What are your views on that? How critical is that, and how can we resolve it?

LaRouche: It's absolutely critical, but the solution is there, if you want to pursue it. The problem is, it's not been pursued. We can get better water. We can get it from Earth, we can get it from the atmosphere of Earth; we can get it even from Mars. But we can also get it from the Galaxy.

In other words the whole system *is* a system! Mankind lives on Earth, within a system, within a system of a much larger range, particularly within the Galactic System, the whole series of galaxies, right? The Galactic System as such. So it's all there. Implicitly, mankind has the ability in practice, in prospect, mankind has the ability to get more and more mastery over essential assets for humanity, for the benefit of humanity, from both our own planet, but from the Solar System. From the history of it.

And therefore the whole system is a mystery, which should not be a mystery. Mankind has had,—coming out of the Twentieth Century in particular,—mankind has had the opportunity of means of developing the use of water and the application of the use of water inside the Galaxy. And therefore, it's only the ignorance of the scientific facts which causes people to feel that they're imprisoned in a dirty water area.

I would say, remove relevant figure in California [Governor Brown], remove him from office, might be a help to clean up the water....

Q: Hi Lyn, how's it going? This is A—.

LaRouche: Well, not too bad. If we get rid of Obama, it'd be excellent.

Time for Mankind to Be Mankind!

Q: [follow-up] We've been doing these different events in Manhattan, as you know. But the one thing, the other day, we went to this Verdi event, in Little Italy. And the guy who gave the presentation, we had discussed the tuning and all the work we have done with Cappuccilli and Bergonzi and all the singers. And what I noticed after discussing with not only the guy who gave the presentation on Verdi, but also the curator at the museum,—is that during the whole speech, they were getting at the question of maintaining the Italian culture in that area.

And when we had discussed what we had done with the Verdi tuning, the guy who ran the museum, and also this guy, had really just lit up and they know that that was what was going to preserve the culture in that region. And one of the guys actually invited us to sing there.

Anyway, that's one part of what we're doing, just to give an idea of how this is shaping here in Manhattan and what you're talking about with using the music question as our edge in Manhattan.

And one thing I want you to elaborate on, is how we're going to take the music work to educate the political work we're doing in the organizing. Because you've been bringing up this idea in different discussions that we've had with you, on this question of use of public speaking for placement, and actually, then, that educating our ability to sing,—but also really I think this question of speech is very crucial for the current culture that we're in right now.

Because you do have a population that just doesn't use irony or metaphor, or any type of elevated speech. And I think that that's part of how we're going to actually get at the top-down fight. Because you do have raise people up from this degenerated culture. And that includes the use of speech.

LaRouche: Well, you're right. You're right. But the question is what is the implication? The implication is that if you merely use arithmetic, or mathematics as it's called—the more elegant term is mathematics—but that is itself the destruction of the cognitive powers of the human individual. And therefore, when you get something like what you referred to *en passant* as the Italian standard,—the Italian standard *is* a correct standard, relative to other standards in Europe and the United States.

And therefore, if you take that as the model, the founding of the Italian system of song, you are touching, right directly, on something that is closer to the human soul than anything else easily available. Get rid of all popular music; destroy it. Don't burn it upwind. [laughter] And therefore, if you get more people who actually have the beautiful song, the beautiful voice of song, that's the right standard to be used. And all of that standard, restore it. That is the correct standard for placing the singing voice *and* the speaking voice!

And that's the weapon to use.

Q: [follow-up] Amen!

LaRouche: If you get the Isle of Manhattan, so to speak, all agreed on the Italian standard for placing of the human voice, you would have a beautiful improvement throughout the nation and beyond. [laughter, applause]

Q: Good afternoon, Mr. LaRouche. I'm P— from the up and coming great state of Connecticut. [laughter] I have a dilemma. It seems that the only way to get through to the congressmen and the senators of our state, Connecticut, is you need constituents. And they literally told me, that if the people aren't complaining, or wanting something, they will do nothing. The example is gun control: They get thousands of letters and emails on gun control.

But Glass-Steagall is not in the language. How do we overcome this?

LaRouche: Well, the time has come, when the use of guns and similar kinds of weapons, is totally counterproductive. Now there has to be some ability to restrain those who would use weapons, like guns or similar weapons, as means of politics, in the political life of society. So the problem is, we have to create and I think we can—look, now, China and India, and Russia and several other nations, are already going in that direction. Curiously for some people, Russia is one of the examples. But the point was, that Putin, who is the present leader of Russia, saw his family killed in defending Europe. Because without Stalin and without

Press Information Bureau of India

Prime Minister Narendra Modi greets school children after addressing the nation on the occasion of the 69th anniversary of India's declaration of independence from the British Empire, on Aug. 15, 2015.

what Stalin provided in defense of Europe against Hitler, and meaning also the United States against Hitler and things like that, or the British. . . . And sometimes the British were really worse than Hitler, because they created Hitler.

So therefore the time when warfare was a way of settling political issues among nations, on similar kinds of issues, has come to an end. Now, that doesn't mean it's just going to come to an end; we have to bring it to an end. Because what we have to do,—we have to not kill people, kill people of nations,—what we have to do is bring some kind of order to the process of the nations. The time has come, when the power of warfare as heretofore known, is impossible! It's intolerable! It cannot happen.

Now, I'm not a pacifist. Because I think if you have to be a pacifist, there's something wrong with you. I don't need to be a pacifist. I know we must not have the use of weaponry of that type, or anything like it, to settle political issues among nations!

Now, for example, we had Obama, Obama, personally, authorized, launched a war against a hospital in the Near East! He did it, willfully, and he proudly did it! He apologized for having done it, but said "there's nothing wrong with what I did." And what Obama did, he plowed over the area where the hospital was being de-

stroyed and the people were being killed, in order to cover up and conceal the details of his crime against that whole population! This is now a matter on the agenda of the international system.

Therefore, you say, we don't want Obama. We don't want him anywhere; the Solar System doesn't want him, the Galaxy doesn't want him, I don't want him. Let's get rid of him.

Just get rid of that whole thing. The time has come for mankind to be mankind! The function of mankind is not warfare! It never really was; but warfare was a means of defense against the British Empire, for example, or against Zeus, earlier. So there have been forces of evil. What must be eliminated is the existence of the force of evil within the realm of mankind. And the time has come that we have the means, the economic means, the physical means, for designing the system which will solve that problem. And therefore, yes, we will now have to maintain a police force, but we don't want to go around killing people forever! What we want to do, is suppress this aspect of man's behavior. And what man may do in harvesting animals and so forth is a different matter.

But mankind is a special being. And mankind is a *uniquely* special being, and therefore man does not eat mankind. We are not cannibals, or anything like it. And therefore, what we have to do, and we can settle it in this period of history, right now, we can begin to settle it from right inside the United States, right now, by throwing Obama out of the Presidency, quickly, immediately.

That would be a good step, because he's the big killer. Obama is the biggest mass killer, operating freely inside the entire United States and beyond! Like what he did in that hospital, in murdering the inmates and medical officials of that hospital. And *he* did it! Not only did he do it, but what he did, he *kept* doing it after he was caught. And the reason he kept doing it, was to hide the evidence against him of what he had done.

So the point is Obama, and what Obama represents, and people like him, people of the same temperament, the same behavior, like the Saudi Emperor; the British traditional system is a similar evil,—historically an evil. Other parts of the planet, same evil.

The time has come, that the most powerful nations in the world in terms of practice, which now include Russia, they include China, they include India, they include a multitude of nations, whose peoples would want to be free of this kind of slaughter,—and the time has come that we have to make... At *this* time, at *this* time!—on the case of Obama, we say the case of Obama's being thrown out of office is a *step* to assure the end of this system of international warfare.

Q: [follow-up] Thank you. Would you consider running for Vice President?
LaRouche: I'm not for vices. [laughter]

Speed: We're going to stop at this point, because both due to our technical glitch and other time constraints, we've got to conclude.

I want to just point out something. Obviously, Lyn,

So, You Wish to Learn All About Economics?

A Text on Elementary Mathematical Economics

by Lyndon H. LaRouche, Jr.

Lyndon LaRouche's university textbook on national economic policy, which also serves as a manual for government officials and advisors to governments.

Downloadable Kindle file $9.95
http://www.larouchepub.com
Product Code: BFBBK-1984-3-0-0-KINDLE

you've said a couple of things: Your proposal concerning Einstein and scientific teaching in Manhattan, and your proposal about the Italian standard of music in Manhattan, and of course, I think I have a better idea now of what you mean by the "Manhattan Party," because we're already having a pretty good time here. So I'd just like to invite you to give us a summary statement, and then we'll conclude.

LaRouche: All right. The time has come for the people of the United States who are now being abused, under the flag of Obama in particular, and other dirty flags which I don't want to mention; the stink is too much.... But the point is, the time has come that we have to now, as in this location, in this particular room and so forth, we have to launch an effort, which actually takes Manhattan as a central reference point for the organization and creation of the United States; and we have to take that authority of Manhattan, or the trust that's embodied in it, as the instrument which we are going to demand be the instrument of authority, of decision, in the immediate period ahead.

Obama has created a wave of evil of his own deeds, which exceeds all precedents in the United States, except actual warfare in the United States itself. He's a man who should have been thrown out a long time ago; he should never even have been born, because the poor fellow, when he was a child, was trained by an evil man; and the stepfather was so evil that the mother of Obama took her son and moved him to the direction of the main states of the United States. But unfortunately, before that movement occurred, Obama had been indoctrinated in *pure Satanic evil*, and I do mean *literally, precisely* Satanic evil, as mankind sometimes does. And that's the case.

Therefore, if you want to get free, if you want to save mankind, you will remove,—lawfully, you will remove Obama from occupying any position of authority. [applause]

Speed: OK, Lyn, thank you very much. And we'll see you, I am certain (though you may not be), next week.
LaRouche: I think I intend to be! [laughter] That's the best I can give you.

Speed: I told you, I'm certain of it! OK, thank you very much.
LaRouche: Have fun!

LaRouche: Democratic Debate Was a Fraud!

Excerpts from Lyndon La-Rouche's telephonic Fire-side Chat of Thursday, Oct 15, hosted by John Ascher.

LaRouche: Well, first of all, the event which happened on Tuesday [Oct 13] of this week, was a general fraud. Now, Hillary Clinton was, of course, the chief fraud in the whole thing, but Obama was also behind it; and you had some other people, who were also of doubtful morals, who were chief operations people in this thing, and behind it was a team of British agents which I intervened on, indirectly,—but intervened on them,—last Friday [Oct 9].

youtube

CNN anchor Anderson Cooper presided over the infamous Oct. 13 Democratic debate according to the British script.

And we knew that the British had set the whole thing up. The entire idea of fundraising, or so forth that was going on out there, was essentially a general fraud. And the people who were listed as the players, as the candidates, so-called, were actually suckered in. And probably, maybe two or three of them, not always the people you might choose, will survive this operation.

My question in this matter, is who's going to survive? Is Hillary going to survive? Because what's happened now really has built her lack of credibility, to the point that she could be knocked out permanently as a candidate. She's gone too far with "El Cheapo" swindles that will probably set up a public reaction of resentment against her. But there are other aspects which are extremely important.

But the thing right now, is that thing was a fraud. It was set up by an organization which had no business trying to run a Presidential event like this; the swindlers who did it are well-known to me personally, and they are swindlers. And the swindlers ran the operation. And the suckers were taken in.

Ascher: I know everybody wanted to know what you had to say about that. I'm going to turn on our Q&A queue. And we will probably get some reports also from the Days of Action this week on the question of reinstating Glass-Steagall, so I imagine we will hear some reports from around the country, Lyn.

Q1: Hi, C— from Boston. I was wondering, I know that you were talking about the Democratic debates that happened this week. But I saw something on the news today, and I was wondering if you had some information, or could comment on it. They were talking about the Lockerbie Pan Am plane crash in 1988, and they're saying they know who did that. I was wondering if there's some backstory to that, or something they're not telling us.

LaRouche: The issue essentially is this fake debate—on a fake call for candidates for President. That system was set up by an operation, and it was actually backed,—which I found out about Friday at noontime,—was actually run by the British Empire. And it was the British Empire agents operating within relevant areas in Texas and that climate-area; and a whole bunch of British agents were out there, staging what was done by a faker who set up the whole operation.

So there was nothing Constitutional about the character of that event. And you have to look at the thing: Here you have a whole hooting bunch of idiots, screaming and yelling like the devil, taking a bunch of candidates and separating them in terms of their role. And the whole thing was occupying a great deal of time, relative to the whole proceedings. The discussion was disgusting; it had no relationship whatsoever to truth, and it was run by people who were, in my view, crooks. So this was not a

U.S. government campaign; it was a racket, which a bunch of people who thought they were candidates, were sucked into.

Ascher: Lyn, we've received a number of questions which we've combined, largely from Facebook, from the Internet; some people have taken your assessment that the Democratic Party debate was a farce, and that the candidates acted as stooges, as an endorsement of their fears—that the whole process is rigged, but that you can't do anything about it.

What do you say could be different about the situation?

LaRouche: First of all, I wouldn't allow that thing to happen. Because the way it was set up, and the arrangement of the whole setup, was a fraud, from beginning to end. The key fraudster was Hillary Clinton. She was the one who played the key role, as the sucker, the official sucker in that whole fraud.

Now, you had a couple of candidates in there, who were actually candidates, several of them,—the two leading ones, and some others who should be considered serious. But otherwise, the whole thing was one giant fraud. And Obama was one of the players in rigging this operation; at least he was the guy who made a speech to authorize it.

But what was done, was done on a private interest, with backing of the British agents who were imported into that territory for that period, at least no later than Friday. So on Friday, I knew the British were running that operation. This was not a U.S. operation, it was a British operation. And people got sucked into this thing.

Now, the whole thing,—if you look at the way the whole proceeding was run,—it was a bunch of lunatics, hollering lunatics, hollering without articulation, hollering without any mental processes visible in that mob. It was a very large mob and it was howling all the time. The whole procedure was disgusting; it was immoral, in the worst, most extreme sense; and it was something that should never have been allowed to happen.

We're going to have a serious election, not a sideshow, not a clowns' sideshow.

Music and Manhattan

Q3: This is W— from Virginia. Mr. LaRouche, when you speak of this process [in musical performance] that occurs "between the notes," when I was

Schiller Institute

The great Italian tenor Carlo Bergonzi (1924 - 2014) gives a master class in New York City under the auspices of the Schiller Institute in 1993. Bergonzi performed at the New York Metropolitan opera at least 300 times over his career.

listening to the Democratic debates—if that's what you want to call them—I definitely figured out pretty quickly that there wasn't anything that was occurring in *that* process between the notes. It was actually on the contrary; they were just being so mechanistic.

Ever since I became aware of this process, you know, I've been listening to a lot of [Wilhelm] Furtwängler's conducting of the works of Brahms, and Bach, and Schumann, and it's amazing! It makes you think. Whereas when you listen to other conductors, where it might sound nice, it just sounds a lot like what we were getting with the Democratic debate. And I was just wondering if you could speak more about that.

LaRouche: Well, sure. We are working on that, actually, significantly especially centered in Manhattan, because Manhattan has the greatest concentration—Manhattan and its immediate vicinities, has the greatest concentration—of great musicians, who are actually qualified, superior concert musicians.

And what has happened recently, is that in the processes which have now developed, we are having a recovery of the real, qualified, Classical musical concept, based on the most famous director in music, [Carlo Bergonzi] from Italy. And he's now of course deceased, but I have a deep memory, because I spent a good deal of time in Italy on that and other interests. And so we had a European and American tradition, but especially centered in Manhattan and around Manhattan. Manhattan has attracted a great number of great musicians, because of the celebrity of Manhattan itself.

So what we have now is a base organization of

people as great musicians, who have great musical talent, and others who are not necessarily great musicians, but are competent musicians.

And this is the basis on which we should use our nation as a whole, as like an audience, a place where people go to celebrate this great event, which is the next Presidential election in the United States. And at that point, if we take the proper approach, the proper cultural approach that's required, we can actually change the situation now. And that means not only the change in the particular situation we're talking about in terms of economy, but in general.

When we look at what has happened to the people of the United States since I was on the team of Ronald Reagan, which I was on for a number of years, and from about that time on, and from the period of Bill Clinton, who also played a credible role in chief, actually—and still represents that today—but apart from that, our nation has been driven down, into garbage. And especially the Bush family garbage producer, and the Obama garbage producer, and also, of course, Cheney, the worst beast of them all!

Our Power to Awaken Mankind

Q5: Hi Lyn, it's B— from L.A. The last time I spoke to you, I spoke on the basis of the spirit of mankind: How do you actually awaken it? And you made it clear that we have the tools to understand humanity.

I was reading some of Nicholas of Cusa's *De Docta Ignorantia*, and the reason why I bring this up is that, in the past weeks there were incidents of putting myself out there and getting a devilish (shall we say) reaction, because we bring up the concept of the future.

I got an interview with a talk show host on Monday, and the direction of the discussion was leaning towards the future. We got a call-in from a person who basically was pessimistic: he was so angry that he couldn't calm down to see that he could actually do something, like the implementation of Glass-Steagall, or thinking of a credit system. But it was a case of the interaction of trying to organize the population so they see themselves as a vehicle to lead mankind, and to actually progress, in such a way that they see that they themselves and others around them, could actually be forced to move mankind into the direction that we did *not* see at all in the Democratic debate, so-called.

For our team on the ground in Las Vegas, and for me, it was like what you just said about how everything was—even before the debate started, you had these protesters—everything was just fake, all around! And the only real thing was our intervention on some of these people, in talking to them, and you could tell they needed leadership! They needed an awakening in themselves to see that they needed to take responsibility. Nobody else will actually do that except themselves....

I can give them a briefing, you know, as in some of my interventions with others, but without conveying the role of Manhattan, it just seems as if none of these interventions are effective. In order to bring mankind out of their dark age mentality ... it just seems like we have to ignite the power to get everybody onboard with you, your conception.

I want to get your response if you can.

LaRouche: Sure. The point is, I think the keystone is the fact that Manhattan is still the center of recruiting people into the United States—the fact that this has been the chief point of mobilization for citizens of the United States, or people who *became* citizens, and that is very important. The number of competent citizens who became citizens there, and who became part of the stream of families which gathered around Manhattan, and had the effect of their influence in New Jersey, in other places and other parts of the East Coast, and into California, especially northern California, and the farm section of California,—these were very important things.

What has happened is the character of those colonizations, from then, in the past up to now, has been discouraged. Why? Well, it's obvious. When you have Bushes elected to be President, for example, and then you had some bad people like Obama, along with the Bushes, and you think of the number of years that Bushes occupied the dominant position in the Presidency of the United States, despite what Bill Clinton did....

And then look at what the Bushes came back to do; and what came out of Obama, who is the most evil and most Satanic of all those Presidents, and still is the embodiment of Satan himself. He's a killer; he kills people! He kills them arbitrarily; he has a kill score. He appoints people to be killed, citizens of the United States to be killed, on his caprice!

Well! The time has come to dump any memory of Obama, and to pay no attention to the claims of the Bushes. And taking that as the top of the list of miscreants, I would say that we've got a pretty good perspective, if we can pull ourselves together and *remember what this nation is and was,* as Alexander Hamilton, in particular, exemplified that.

Ascher: B—, who just asked Mr. LaRouche that question, was involved about a week ago in a major intervention at a big political event in Los Angeles, which was followed by the radio show that he referenced. And then this past Tuesday, B— was also part of our team out at the hall in Las Vegas where the Democratic Party debate took place.

Our Goal: the Highest Level

Q9: Hello, my name is E—, from Columbia, Maryland. My question is, during the Democratic debate they did mention Glass-Steagall, but it was only from two candidates. The other two, they should have said something. If you had to vote, would you support O'Malley or Bernie Sanders? And it was Bernie Sanders who believes in the idea of socialism.

LaRouche: Bernie Sanders, to my knowledge, is not an appropriate choice of candidate for President of the United States. O'Malley is a different case. O'Malley is a man who has intrinsic honesty in the way the history of his politics has been; and everything I know about him is honorable. There are possibly other people who should be considered.

At this point, people usually think, we want *a* President. Now, according to our national law, we do get a President, *a* President, one President. We also get a Vice President, and we hope he's not a President of Vice.

But then, on the other hand, what we need is a *team* of citizens who are qualified to lead the formation and institution of a system of government under a Presidential system. In other words, you can't just say, "this is the President, now everybody's going to listen to him." That's not right.

You have to have a President who is acceptable, who's qualified to lead the nation. But no one person can control the United States as a nation efficiently. There has to be a team, based on the kind of team that we have when we compose a Presidential system. It also means we depend on the way we can deal with our members of Congress in the House of Representatives in general, and so forth.

So we need that office, of people who don't always agree with each other, but we need that kind of office as a deliberation process, in order to have the people of the United States find that they have a core of agreement on goals and purposes which suit the requirements of the Presidency.

Now, the other part of that is—it has another feature

youtube

The Democratic cadidate debate was a fraud, LaRouche stated. "Clinton was the chief fraud in the whole thing, but Obama was also behind it."

to it—when we try to create a Presidential system, we don't try to create a Presidential system *per se*; we try to incorporate the best features of our existence and our history; our intention is to introduce *new* conceptions, more appropriate conceptions, more brilliant, more fruitful, than any team before. There may be some who are only rivals. But our goal is to go to the highest level of achievement of the improvement of our system of government, and create a team of people who are qualified, and actively qualified, to conduct the business of our government as a whole.

And that's the way we have to look at it.

Go Beyond 'My Nation'

Q10: This is R— in Oregon, and concurrent with what Mr. LaRouche just said, I think we'd like to see a vision of collegiality come back to the Executive Office. We've had enough of this so-called unilateral executive agency which really turns out to be not much more than just a curtain, behind which Britain gets to manipulate the Presidency.

But my question was, there's been a lot of talk over the last 10 years or so about reinstating Glass-Steagall, and now you've got the BRICS system pretty much underway, Mr. LaRouche. And I wonder if the BRICS agreements that are taking place, if they're going to supplant the need for a New Bretton Woods conference, which we often used to hear about. Or whether currency exchange agreements are part of the BRICS banking proposals, or if you're still going to need a New Bretton Woods conference as one of the items on your agenda?

LaRouche: I think one of the key things on the

agenda is Glass-Steagall. Because if you have a money system which is not in accord, or similarity, with Glass-Steagall, you're not going to have a modern society which is qualified to function for the benefit of any nation.

So we have a change which is now in process, a global change in progress which is not yet generally discussed in the United States, but it's a very important consideration. What we have now is that China is the greatest nation on the planet. That's a fact. The rise of China, again—because it did have a rise and fall at various points—but China is the most powerful nation, in terms of people, on this planet right now.

Now, there's also India with over a billion people; and they are a power, and they will become a power under the current new leadership, if it's continued. And we find that also, in the course of this, we can affect nations which are now in great quarrels with each other. We find that it's possible for us, as Putin has demonstrated for the area he's operating in now, to demonstrate that we can make peace, where strife and bloody strife has been a problem.

These changes will occur. The idea of national sovereignties, and the protection of individual national sovereignties, is a required achievement. But mankind is not just a collection of competing states. These different states have different colorations, in terms of their history and their character. But eventually, as we see in South America, in the best developments in South America, and in other places, we find out that the idea of "my nation as itself, for itself" is not acceptable. We must have national standards which are *our* national standards, but which lead into an efficient accord with other nations. In other words, our sovereignty is our sovereignty; we will not give it up easily. And more exactly will not give it up; we don't have to. Because we will find that we will go into more and more stages of international cooperation.

And therefore, what we want to do is take that idea. Use that for the United States, to revive the United States from the mess it's become, and build a kind of system back in the United States, our Presidential system, our Constitutional system, and make that work for a change! It did work at times in the past. We now have to make it work, and we have to make it work as being a part of a family of nations which are seeking to

Petr Pavlicek/IAEA

China at the Forefront: Chinese scientists in the control room of the experimental high temperature gas-cooled reactor at Tsinghua University, Beijing in June 2004.

find ways not only to cooperate, but to make achievements which take the power of man beyond the limits of the Solar System, and into areas which are beyond, the larger part of the system.

So the time has come for us to realize that the accelerated advances in technology,—creative technology, not the usual stuff,—but that kind of development is the future of mankind. And you find that in the case of China, for example; there is a mood in China now, at an accelerating rate—that doesn't mean it's perfect, but it means an accelerating rate—it's a leading nation on the planet and it's moving in a direction which seeks cooperation with such as our United States and other nations in that group.

So we have to understand, we have to have an honest and truthful vision of where mankind—where the nations of mankind—must go, how they must achieve new levels of cooperation and efficiency. And that's what we ought to concentrate on.

A Beautiful Devotion

Q11: Lyn, I have a question which is somewhat similar to the theme that you just brought up. This is from M— in Dearborn, Michigan. He says, "I have noticed that there have been many meetings between Israel and Russia lately, and Saudi Arabia and Russia. My question is, what is being discussed in these meetings? Is it just short-term—how to stop terrorism and prevent wars from expanding? Or is there also a discussion of mutually beneficial relationships that can create a lasting peace in this region based on real, universal principles? Also, is China involved in this discussion? Thanks very much."

LaRouche: China's very much involved in these matters. My wife is very familiar with a lot of the important details of what has happened in China over much of her lifetime in particular. And that kind of development,—as in Russia today: Russia, for example, revived itself from the tumult and trials it went through. And Putin has brought the thing into order. I wouldn't say it's perfect order; but I wouldn't say that Putin would say it's a perfect order! But the point is, the idea of the cooperation between Russia now, and with nations in its neighbor-

NASA

"Mankind is already ready to go back to space." Here, Expedition 43 Commander and NASA astronaut Terry Virts prepares camera equipment for an upcoming documentation session from the Space Station's Destiny lab, on June 15, 2015.

hood—its relationship to India, its conspicuous relationship to China, and so forth—this is something which is of precious value, and can lead to that result.

And that's the way we should look at it. Because what we have to do, is we have to understand that the basis,—let me lay this out because this is something which is touchy, but it's also true and I believe in it: The question is, we all are human—we hope! If we're not human, we don't extend that courtesy to other strangers. [chuckles.]

But we know that mankind dies. Every human being dies, on the record so far. And there has been no recipe to say that human beings will not sooner or later die. Well, you say, what's the meaning, then, of human beings, if they're going to die? If that's the trash-end of life, as it might be called.

The point is, if we as human beings develop what we call technologies,—by which I mean really scientific technologies, *real* scientific technologies, not gimmicks,—then mankind is capable and has the power, and we know—as those of us who are in on, shall we say, the scientific history—we know that mankind is not going to be confined to living on Earth.

Now, we don't know all the complications that involves, but we know that what mankind is able to achieve—as mankind, for the future of mankind, for the human species, for the *meaning* of the human species as a continuing process—depends upon a process of development. It's not just a process of getting rich. It's a pro-

cess of achieving something which is greater than had ever been achieved before. That's the mission of life.

We all live. We will all die. There is no known exception to that rule. But if we have lived in the proper way, and devoted our living in the proper direction, then we have an answer,—an opportunity of an answer,—to go out beyond the bounds of Earth as such, and realize that mankind is already ready to go back to space; despite Obama, we're going back to space. We're going to do things about Mars, we're going to do things about other things.

Why? For a joy ride? No! Because we know that we have to deal with the challenges which are embedded in the existence of the planetary systems like the Solar System, the Galaxy,—these things cannot be ignored. Even the idea of the Moon, the Moon system, the Earth system, we have to have that.

So mankind is going to depend upon the development of the powers of mankind, which are supplied in increase by the scientific creativity of mankind. And that would tell us that mankind has a beautiful devotion, a devotion to the heavens.

Slap It on His Desk!

Q15: Hi, Mr. LaRouche. This is K— from Massachusetts.... I was calling everybody down in the House of Representatives and the Senate, and they were saying how Obama would never sign his name onto Glass-Steagall. I said, "Then, slap the 25th

Amendment on his desk!"

LaRouche: You got it! That's right! [laughs] That's an absolutely appropriate tactic!

Q15: They said, "How would we do that?" I said, "What d'ya mean, how would you do it? You just have it in your hand, and you slap it on his desk. I know that's what I would do!"

LaRouche: That's a good idea. That's an excellent idea. I think you've got the spirit to know what to do about that.

creative commons/Diliff

The Rose Main Reading Room at the New York City Public Library in Manhattan. The free library has the second largest collection in the United States (after the Library of Congress), and the fourth in the world, as befits Manhattan's status as the cultural capital of the United States. It has more visitors by far than even the larger libraries—18 million a year.

Finding Those Who Want Ideas

Q16: This is T— from Lake Arrowhead, New York. I went to the debate and stood there in the shadow of the golden Trump Tower there, 500 foot tall with gilt windows, and watched one group of suckers going into the casino to lose their money that way, and another group of suckers going into the Democratic [debate] to lose their money and their souls that way.

And I'm watching people go through the motions, and there were a few people—well, there was one particular lady—I was just wandering among Hillary supporters, trying to talk to *somebody*—get through the shouting, you know. And there was one lady standing there, and she didn't have a Hillary shirt on, but she was carrying it. And she seemed open somehow. I handed her your seven-point program, and she told me, "I'm not interested in cheering for a candidate, I want to hear about ideas!"

And I go, "Oh my goodness, have I got the ideas for you!" And then I was able to sell her your full recovery program for five bucks, and your "Join the BRICS" one, so she's someone you could talk to—but one out of how many? I wish I knew how to spot those people or how to get through to them, because I know there's a lot of people there who're just going through the motions; in their heart they know it.

LaRouche: Well, some of us have to take the leadership in a competent way. I'm an old man now, so I

have obviously some more experience than some other people do. Particularly, I've been professional in this whole field anyway.

No, it can be done. It depends upon having teamwork, or creating a teamwork system, which can discover among themselves how to proceed to get their voices heard—and that means being efficiently heard—where people have to turn around and think and listen to what you say, as teamwork. And that works; it will work.

I think that in the case of Manhattan, for example,—which I spend a lot of special attention on, not only because it is Manhattan, but because Manhattan is a leading element in the process of the United States as a whole. If we understand what Manhattan represents in terms of its influence over the nation as a whole, you appreciate that. You don't turn down other parts of the United States as such, but you recognize that Manhattan has a very special authority, since Alexander Hamilton brought the United States into being by his leadership.

So I think that view of Manhattan, as being a central reference point for the nation as a whole, stands pretty well. And from that standpoint, you operate on that basis. Wherever you live, wherever you work, you may have to have a certain respect for Manhattan, because you know it has more influence on the national functions as a whole than any other part of the system.